異國風味

韓國菜
KOREAN
CUISINE

崔英淑　Young Sook Choi

味全食譜
Wei-Chuan Cookbook

作　者：崔英淑
總編輯：黃淑惠
烹飪協助：李銀山

AUTHOR: Young Sook Choi
EDITOR: Su-Huei Huang
DISH PRESENTATION: Eun San Yi

翻　譯：何久恩、賴燕貞
文稿協助：郭書香、馮文潔、王志偉
　　　　　陳素真

TRANSLATION: John Holt, Yen-Jen Lai
EDITORIAL STAFF: Cynthia Kuo, Man-Kit (Jenny) Fong,
Chi-Wai Wong, Su-Jen Chen

攝　影：周唐
封面設計：王瑾
設　計：張菲

PHOTOGRAPHY: Don C. Cho
COVER DESIGN: Chin Ong
DESIGN: Faye Chang

電腦排版：友坤電腦排版
分色製版：大光華印務部
印　刷：錦龍印刷實業股份有限公司

PRINTED IN TAIWAN

版權所有：局版台業字第0179號
2001年5月初版
2005年1月2版　2-2-0

WEI-CHUAN PUBLISHING
1455 Monterey Pass Rd., #110
Monterey Park, CA 91754, U.S.A.
Tel:　323 · 261 · 3880 ▪ 323 · 261 · 3878
Fax: 323 · 261 · 3299
www.weichuancookbook.com

7 16598 00080 2

FIRST PRINTING: MAY 2001
2nd　PRINTING: JAN 2005
ISBN 0-941676-80-3

目錄 · CONTENTS

崔 英淑女士是美國知名韓式連鎖餐廳"又來屋"的第二代經營者。在 80 年代當崔女士積極的投入管理經營"又來屋"後,便決定配合現代人的需求,讓韓國菜成為一種流行、時尚的餐飲。她以新的經營管理方式讓"又來屋"成功的在美國的主要城市,如洛杉磯、比華利山、紐約均有據點,英國的倫敦分店也將在近期內開幕。

如何健康的烹煮、選擇食材及搭配菜色是崔女士認為韓國菜中十分重要的。為了朝此目標來推廣韓國菜,崔女士專程回到韓國去鑽研韓式料理的精髓,她不僅在各地的市場採購、參觀,也嚐盡各式各樣的美食及地方小吃,足跡遍及韓國每一角落,在更深入地了解韓國菜的豐富及多元化後,她有了強烈的使命感,也為自己能繼承如此富饒的飲食文化而感到自豪。然而她卻也發現傳統美味的韓國菜並沒有使用標準量器,廚師全憑個人的經驗或"嚐嚐看"來決定要放多少份量的材料及調味料,總讓有心想學習韓國菜的人感到十分困惑。

因此,崔女士花了數年的時間去研究,經過無數次的試驗,終於成功的為韓國菜建立了準確而有系統的測量法。也讓"又來屋"的客人在每一家分店,都可享用一樣美味的佳餚。同樣也順利地將一些傳統而美味的韓國菜現代化,進而編寫成這本食譜。

作者感言

這本書包含了我多年來推廣韓國菜的心得經驗,期望藉由本食譜的出版,讓韓國菜可以伸入不同的民族及文化中,和讀者們共同分享及互相交流。同時我也將繼續努力於改良和創新韓國菜,希望有機會可以再出版新的食譜。在此,我衷心感謝顧問 Mr. Elmer Azuma ,比華利山分店主廚李銀山於烹飪上的鼎力協助及所有"又來屋"的顧客多年來給予的支持和鼓勵。

崔英淑

Ms. Young Sook Choi is a second generation family owner and operator of the famous Woo Lae Oak restaurants in the U.S., these restaurants have gone a long way toward popularizing Korean cuisine in the U.S. During the 1980's, when she became more integrally involved in the overall management of the restaurants, she determined it was time to re-evaluate Korean cuisine from a "modern" perspective. Her success can be seen by the growing popularity of her restaurants in major cities - Los Angeles, Beverly Hills, New York, and another expected to open in London.

Specifically, she wished to bring a greater focus on healthy eating and how food should be prepared and presented in Korean restaurants across the country. In order to properly fulfill this desire, she decided to go to the "source". She returned to Korea and traveled through every region, shopping in all the small market places, and dining in many, many local restaurants. This was an educational trip to re-discover the immensely rich, cultural tapestry inherent in Korean cuisine. Her journey into history brought back wonderful childhood memories and re-ignited pride in her Korean heritage. However, from a culinary perspective, she was less than enchanted with her findings. She found there was no system of measurements in Korean cooking. Everything was prepared with "fingertip taste" and "a little bit of spice", two phrases which, unless you are Korean born and bred, have absolutely no meaning whatsoever.

Accordingly, she set about creating a system of measurements through extensive trial and error. After several years of experimentation, she was successful in her quest to create a uniform system of measurements for these ancient recipes. The results of these efforts are now incorporated in this cookbook. Each recipe approximates the "fingertip taste" axiom, while at the same time employing 21st century techniques. In addition, she has refined the "a little bit of every spice" to satisfy the more sophisticated palate.

Author's Comments

I believe that all knowledge must be shared in order to progress. The contents of this book, for which I have made my best efforts through several years, can only be improved with the reader's contributions, and I welcome readers comments in that regard.

I myself, will make a continuous effort to introduce more innovative Korean cuisine through more books. I thank consultant Mr. Elmer for his hard work with me through several years, Chef, Eun Sang Yi for his assistance, dedication and beautiful presentations, and all of our Woo Lae Oak family and customers.

Young Sook Choi

李 銀山大廚的生涯起源於 1987 年起的韓國漢城著名餐廳。之後，他在"又來屋"洛杉磯西城分店任廚服務。 1993 年由 Elmar Komakata 法國烹飪學校畢業後，他便擔任"又來屋"在比華利山分店的主廚。 1999 年開幕的 "又來屋 "紐約蘇荷區分店，也由其負責策劃廚房流程。

Mr. Eun San Yi began his professional career at the Korea Palace, a four star restaurant in Seoul, Korea in 1987. Subsequently, he worked at the Woo Lae Oak restaurant in Los Angeles. After his graduation from the famous French cooking school, Elmar Komakata in 1993, he moved on to the popular Beverly Hills Woo Lae Oak restaurant where he is currently the Executive Chef. Additionally, Chef Yi had been instrumental in establishing and training chefs at the Woo Lae Oak's New York Soho restaurant, which opened in 1999.

韓國菜基本認識
KOREAN CUISINE BASICS

說起韓國菜，總讓人聯想到美味的烤肉、辛辣的泡菜及包羅萬象的小菜；當然香辣的湯煲也同樣讓人食指大動，胃口大開。韓國菜不僅著重於酸、甜、鹹、辣味的搭配，同時也兼顧各方面營養上的均衡。

韓國菜主要的調味料包括海鹽、醬油、糖、米醋、麻油、大蒜、豆瓣及辣椒醬等。菜餚除選用蔬菜、肉類和海鮮為材料外，也常使用豆類製品及南北雜貨如芝麻、松子、栗子、紫菜絲等，而烹調的方式則運用蒸、煮、炒、炸、烤來加以變化。

大量的使用辣椒是韓菜特別之處，如新鮮辣椒、乾辣椒、韓國辣椒粉及辣椒醬都普遍的在韓菜中出現。進餐時，香甜的米飯加上美味的菜餚，搭配開胃的小菜、一碗熱湯或是味道濃郁的煲；就是傳統的韓國菜了。

然而在快速繁忙的工商社會中，準備一餐傳統的韓國菜，又要搭配多樣的小菜和泡菜，是讓人望而卻步的。本書採用創新的烹調方式和簡化的步驟來迎合現代 21 世紀人的需求，不僅保留韓菜的原有風味，更讓您在忙碌的步調中，仍可享用傳統美味的韓國菜。

When one thinks of Korean cuisine, one is reminded of the richly aromatic barbeques, the sumptuous array of cool and spicy pickles, and the deliciously flavored hot stews. Korean food has a long tradition of offering various contrasting flavors, such as salty, sweet, hot and sour. In addition, balancing of colors, textures and nutritional foods, such as vegetables, grains, meat and seafood is also important to the Korean meal.

Korean cuisine is flavored with a combination of sea salt, soy sauce, sugar, rice wine, vinegar, garlic, sesame oil, chili and soybean paste; cooked mainly by grilling, steaming, stir-frying, deep-frying, and boiling. Furthermore, toasted sesame seeds, pine nuts, chestnuts, seaweed and soy products are used extensively in Korean cuisine.

Korean cuisine is distinct from other Asian cuisines in its liberal use of chilies, including fresh, dried, powdered, and also as paste (*go chu jang*). The wonderfully abundant choices of side dishes (*panchan*) and pickled foods, most notably (*kimchi*) are a part of nearly every meal. They are intended to enhance one's appetite and add to the enjoyment of the entire meal. Crunching a bit of spicy Kimchi, nibbling a bit of steamed rice, picking a bit of cool cucumber and slurping a bit of hot soup; this range and diversity characterizes Korean's unique way of maintaining a balance of foods and flavors in their daily diet.

Preparing an authentic Korean meal in an increasingly fast-paced world can be a daunting task, especially when one chooses to serve the many small side dishes (panchan) traditionally accompanying each meal. However, this cookbook offers simplified recipes and techniques which effectively adapt and redevelop Korean traditions to reflect the aesthetics of the 21st century, thus preserving these timeworn, century old culinary mores for future generations.

韓國人的主食

韓國人的主食為米飯，多選用蓬萊米。此種呈橢圓形的米；煮熟後較黏。不同種類的米，主要分別在於其不同的味道及口感；選擇米種時依照個人喜好即可。韓國人也會將米與其它穀類如豆、小米等混合一起煮食；粥、麵及麵粉餅有時也可取代米飯做為主食。

KOREAN STAPLES The primary staple in Korean cuisine is rice, and in particular, medium-to-short grained rice. This is a rice of rounded white kernels that when cooked, become moist and slightly stickier than the long grain rice most Americans are familiar with. Depending on the preferences of the individual, different kinds of rice will produce various tastes and textures. In addition to rice, the Korean meal staple may also consist of other grains, porridge, noodles and flour pancakes.

韓國泡菜

(Kimchi) 在韓文中意思為醃製的食品，一般通稱為泡菜，材料用大白菜、白蘿蔔、紅蘿蔔、小黃瓜、活蟹、明蝦及蠔等。在有現代化科技和便捷交通之前，一般家庭會在寒冷的冬季來臨之前，一次醃製大量各種不同的泡菜，以便慢慢食用。以大白菜所製成的泡菜俗稱為韓國泡菜，是韓國人最喜愛的一種泡菜，作法是將大白菜先用鹽及醋醃；再把每一片白菜均勻灑上蒜、薑、和韓國辣椒粉後讓其發酵。此種美味的韓國泡菜做起來費時，且製成品在大多數超市均有販售，所以本書內將不再特別介紹其製作細節。

KIMCHI is a Korean term applied to various preserved foods. Before the advent of modern transportation and technology, preserving food was a necessity due to the harsh winter weather in the region. Large portions are prepared for multiple servings over extended periods. Kimchi is considered a national dish, and cabbage Kimchi has been for a long time, the Korean's favorite dish. The making of this favorite is very complex and requires that Napa cabbage be marinated with salt and vinegar; each layer sprinkled with garlic, ginger and red pepper powder, then fermented. This complex process is no longer necessary since ready-made Kimchi may be purchased in most super markets, or even convenience stores. In addition to cabbages, a wide variety of vegetables and seafoods can be made into kimchi: daikon, carrots, cucumbers, garlic, live crabs, prawns, oysters.

小菜

通常是將材料以生醃、川燙或快炒後再調味的方式處理。和費時費力製成的泡菜相比，小菜的烹調方法較為簡易。小菜的種類很多，本書內所介紹的是較為普遍的韓國小菜。

SIDE DISHES (PANCHAN) They are either served raw or lightly blanched or stir-fried before seasonings are added. The preparation of these side dishes is much easier than the procedures involved in preparing Kimchi. While there are innumerable side dishes, this cookbook covers those that are most popular and commonly served.

湯·煲　湯所使用的材料比煲少，有時高湯內僅灑些蔥花即可當湯，通常與別的菜餚一起上桌，無法單獨配飯為一餐。煲內所使用的材料份量較多，湯汁剛好蓋滿材料即可，材料可用豆腐、泡菜、蔬菜、肉類及海鮮等。煲通常用石頭鍋烹煮，有的味道刺激辛辣，很下飯。連鍋上桌，可單獨配飯當餐，也可搭配其他菜餚食用。

湯及煲通常用牛高湯或魚高湯做為湯頭。

SOUPS (*KOK · TANG*) AND **STEWS** (*CHIGE*)　may range from a light seafood soup with ingredients such as seaweed, clams, or a simple clear beef broth with a sprinkle of minced green onions to a heavier soupy stew with tofu, kimchi, vegetables, meat and seafood in pungent and mouth-burning spicy flavors. Cooked and served in stone pots, stews use more ingredients with liquid just covering and are generally served with steamed rice. Stews may be served as one dish meals or as another dish to be shared by everyone at the table.

Beef broth and anchovy stock are often used as a foundation upon which to build soups and stews.

牛高湯

將 ① 料用中火煮滾，續煮 1 小時後去雜質及牛骨。加入 ② 料再煮滾約 1 分鐘。可得 10 杯。

① ┌ 牛排骨………1 斤半(900 克)
　 └ 水 ……………………15 杯

② ┌ 鹽………………………1 小匙
　 │ 韓國醬油(見 14 頁)…2 大匙
　 └ 牛肉精(見 14 頁) …1/4 小匙

BEEF BROTH

Boil ① over medium heat for 1 hour then clarify the broth. Add ②, boil for another minute.
Makes about 10 cups

① ┌ 2 lb. (900g) short ribs
　 └ 15 c. water

② ┌ 1 t. salt
　 │ 2 T. Korean soy sauce (p.14)
　 └ ¼ t. beef bouillon (p.14)

魚高湯

將 ① 料用中火煮滾 20 分鐘後去雜質。

① ┌ 魚乾(見 13 頁)………10 隻
　 │ 海帶(昆布)(見 11 頁)
　 │ 　 10x10 公分 ………1 張
　 │ 白蘿蔔(2.5x5 公分)……1 塊
　 └ 水 …………………………10 杯

ANCHOVY STOCK

Boil ① over medium heat for 20 minutes then clarify the stock.

① ┌ 10 dried anchovies (p.13)
　 │ 1 seaweed (dashima) (p.11), 4"x4"
　 │ 　 (10x10cm)
　 │ 1 piece radish, 1" x 2" (2.5x5cm)
　 └ 10 c. water

去除雜質的秘訣　熬煮高湯時，要將浮在湯面上的泡沫撈出。煮好後，用鋪有細紗布的濾網過濾，放入冰箱內，再把凝固的浮油拿掉，就可有完全無油、澄清的高湯。

Tips for clarifying broth and stock: During cooking, regularly skim off scum rising to the surface. After the stock/broth is made, pour through a strainer lined with a cheese-cloth or fine cotton cloth. The stock/liquid may be fully degreased by refrigerating until the fat solidifies, making removal easy.

炒　炒菜時若用大火，需動作快、時間短，才可保留食物的營養、顏色、味道及口感。如有需要醃、切或加調味汁，都需在烹調前準備好。先將鍋及油預熱，再放入材料，烹調時間較長的材料要先下鍋。若使用不粘鍋，則用少量的油就可達到相同的效果，可做為健康烹調的選擇。

STIR-FRYING *(BOKGUM)*　Stir-frying should be short and quick in order to retain the nutritional value of the foods as well as their colors, flavors and textures. All the neccesary marinating, chopping, slicing, seasoning sauces should be made prior to stir-frying. The key is to preheat the wok and oil then stir-fry over very high heat. Always begin with the ingredients that require longest cooking time. Nonstick frying pans or woks are particularly useful for the health conscious cook, since they allow frying with little oil.

特殊用具及量器介紹
SPECIAL EQUIPMENT AND MEASURING TOOLS

桌上型瓦斯爐及烤架　韓國人喜愛在餐桌上煮食，不但可保持食物熱度，也增加進食的樂趣。室內燒烤時，在桌上型瓦斯爐上置烤架點火後，就可燒烤肉類、海鮮或蔬菜。煮煲時，也可直接將煮食鍋放上。這種桌上型瓦斯爐及烤架可在一般的亞洲超市內購得。

Table Top Burner and Metal Grids　Koreans love cooking foods at the table. Not only will the foods always stay hot, it is also fun to eat as the food is being cooked. Primarily used for barbequing indoors, the burner is fueled by a disposable and replaceable butane gas canister. All may be purchased at most Asian markets.

石頭鍋　一般用來煮煲或煲仔飯，有保存食物熱度的功能，通常煮好後直接連鍋上桌。韓國人在寒冷的冬季時，特別喜愛非常燙的食物，故煮煲時常直接在桌上煮食。

Stone Pot　Primarily used to cook stews. With the use of a portable table top burner, they can be cooked and served directly at the table. Koreans love their foods piping hot, especially during the cold winters. These pots serve the purpose; once heated through, they will retain heat for a long time.

1 杯（1 飯碗）=16 大匙	1 大匙（1 湯匙）	1 小匙（1 茶匙）
1 c. (1 cup) = 236 c.c.	**1 T.** (1 Tablespoon) = 15 c.c.	**1 t.** (1 teaspoon) = 5 c.c.

給讀者的小交代　量調味料時，請用標準量器。所有食譜內的材料，除有特別指示外，均為洗過、削皮後或處理過的淨重。

Tips for Using This Book　When measuring ingredients, fill measuring tools until full, then level. Unless specified, all the ingredients listed in the recipes are washed, peeled, prepared, and the weights used are net weights.

常用材料介紹
FREQUENTLY USED INGREDIENTS

1 **麵線** 是亞洲麵條中最細的一種，可以冷或熱食。韓國有名的冷食是將煮好的麵線放入冰豆漿內或加醬涼拌，熱食吃法與中國式差不多，即把煮好的麵線加入熱湯料內。

2 **冬粉** 是以綠豆澱粉及馬鈴薯粉製成的透明粉絲，故又名粉絲或細粉。書內所用的是較粗的冬粉，使用時將多量水燒開熄火，放入冬粉浸泡 5 分鐘至軟，再用水漂涼瀝乾即可。冬粉本身無味，需與其他的材料或調味品一起烹煮。

3 **糯米** 比一般的米粒有黏性，糯米可做成小吃或甜點亦可與其他穀類混合煮成"五穀飯"。糯米粉是將糯米磨成的粉。

4 **栗子** 有新鮮、乾的或罐裝的。栗子用途廣泛，除了煮成泥當甜點餡料外，還可加在糯米飯內或與肉燒煮。．

5 **松子** 含有豐富蛋白質及脂質。松子除平常當零嘴外，亦可放入粥內或用來作為盤飾。

1 **Somen** Resembling Italian angel hair pasta, somen is perhaps the thinnest Asian noodle available. This fine and delicate noodle is made from white flour. Somen can be cooked and served chilled in a bowl of soybean broth or with a dipping sauce. However, somen may also be served hot in soup.

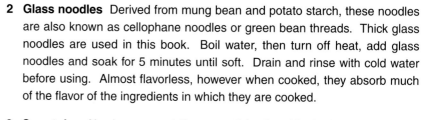

2 **Glass noodles** Derived from mung bean and potato starch, these noodles are also known as cellophane noodles or green bean threads. Thick glass noodles are used in this book. Boil water, then turn off heat, add glass noodles and soak for 5 minutes until soft. Drain and rinse with cold water before using. Almost flavorless, however when cooked, they absorb much of the flavor of the ingredients in which they are cooked.

3 **Sweet rice** Also known as glutinous or sticky rice, this rice has a high starch content. When cooked, it becomes stickier than the everyday medium-grain rice. It is often used with a mixture of grains or as an ingredient in many sweets and snacks. Sweet rice flour is derived from sweet rice.

4 **Chestnuts** Whether fresh, dried or canned, Koreans like to use them not only in sweet desserts, but also cook them with meat or as an ingredient in rice dishes.

5 **Pine nuts** Rich in protein and lipids, they are eaten as a snack, ground up in porridge or used as an attractive garnish. Broad coned pine nuts tend to have a stronger flavor than the slender and delicately flavored pine nuts.

6 炒芝麻　將芝麻在無油的鍋內以中火炒至淡黃色；炒過的芝麻很香，用途廣泛，可與其他調味料拌和當醃料及沾料，亦可與蔬菜涼拌或當盤飾等。

7 紫菜　又稱海苔，含有豐富的鈣質、維他命及礦物質，香脆中帶點海洋風味。市場有很多不同品質及尺寸的紫菜，因怕受潮一般裝在真空處理過的塑膠或錫罐內出售。紫菜的用途為包飯、灑在飯上或湯內當調味料，另外也可用作為盤飾。

8 海帶　又名"昆布"，是將一種天然海草晒乾的製成品，煮高湯時加入可增加鮮味。其它用途與海帶芽相同。

　　海帶芽　是一種較嫩的天然海草晒乾所製成，泡水後即可用來炒、涼拌或加入湯內。

9 高麗參　一種像人形的根類植物，一般人認為有很好的藥效，依品質其價位也有差異。高麗參除泡茶喝外，可製人蔘烤醬及烹煮〝人蔘雞〞。

10 薑　帶有刺激性及微辣的味道，一般作為辛香料。老薑比嫩薑辣，嫩薑宜放入冰箱內保存，老薑放在陰涼處即可。

6 Toasted sesame seeds are used extensively as a seasoning in marinades, sauces and vegetable side dishes as well as an attractive garnish. Toasting brings out the full aroma and flavor of the seeds. To toast, stir continuously in a dry pan over medium heat until they turn slightly golden.

7 Seaweed (kim) Korean "kim," also known by the Japanese name "nori," are paper-thin sheets of dried seaweed. They are crisp, with a delicate marine taste, rich in iodine, vitamins and minerals. They are sold in a wide variety of sizes ranging from large sheets to bundles of short toasted strips. They are packaged in airtight plastic or tin canisters to avoid moisture. "Kim" is used to wrap sushi or rice; toasted short strips are great as a seasoning or garnish when sprinkled over soups or rice dishes.

8 Seaweed (dashima) is sun-dried kelp, often known by its Japanese name "kombu". It dispenses a fresh ocean flavor to foods and is primarily used as a flavoring agent for stock. It comes in thick, stiff sheets with a powdery, salty finish.

Seaweed (*miyuk*) is sun-dried kelp, it should be soaked in water before cooking. It can be treated as a vegetable, added to soups, stews or stir-fry dishes.

9 Ginseng root Widely regarded as a rejuvenating herb, Koreans ascribe much medicinal power to this famous root. Prices range from the astronomical figures for the finest grade to a small fraction of that price for a low-grade ginseng. In addition to tea, ginseng may be cooked with foods, such as in stuffed chicken, or simmered in soy sauce to make a dressing.

10 Ginger Used often as a spice, the mature ginger is spicier and more pungent than young ginger. Since young ginger has a lighter taste and may be substituted for more mature ginger, you may wish to increase the amount. In most cases, ginger should be peeled before shredding, mincing, etc.

11 韓國辣椒 為細長微辣的綠色辣椒，成熟時會轉成漂亮的鮮紅色。辣椒的種類很多，若無韓國辣椒，依自己的喜愛選擇即可。

12 白蘿蔔 含有大量維他命及助消化的酵素，白蘿蔔在韓國菜的用法與中國菜相同，可涼拌生吃，爛煮、紅燒、煮湯或雕刻作為盤飾。

13 黃豆芽／綠豆芽 二者均有爽口的白色莖部，可炒、涼拌或煮湯，最大的分別在於前者為大黃豆的種子，後者為綠豆小芽，而黃豆芽不能生吃。

14 大白菜 是亞洲蔬菜中很常用的一種白菜，可醃成泡菜、切碎後作為餃子餡、也可油炒或煮湯。

15 韓國西洋菜 一種生長在水中的植物，注意烹調時間不宜過長，若用於煮湯，可用唐好菜取代。

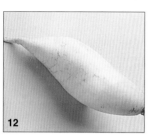

11 Korean Chili Peppers are skinny, long and mildly spicy. When ripe, Korean chili peppers turn to a beautiful, bright red. They can also be sliced into thin threads as an attractive garnish. Jalapeno, a spicier, rounder and wider green chilli, is more readily available in American markets and makes a fine substitute.

12 Daikon (white radish) Substantially larger and milder than the small red radish that most Americans are familiar with, this giant white radish is known to be rich in vitamins and high in beneficial digestive enzymes. The radish is used and prepared in various ways. It is dressed and eaten raw as a side dish, sliced and shredded in stir-fries, stews, soups, and pickled or grated in dipping sauce, Furthermore, it can also be carved or shredded as an attractive garnish.

13 Soybean／Mung Bean Sprouts are known for their high protein content. Both have crunchy white stems, however, soybean sprouts are distinguished from the mung bean sprouts by their large yellow soybean seed heads as opposed to tiny bud-like green heads. While mung bean sprouts are sometimes served raw, soybean sprouts should never be served raw. Both may be stir-fried, cooked in broth, or parboiled and dressed as a vegetable side dish.

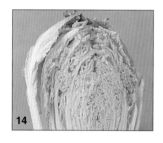

14 Napa Cabbage Also called Korean or Chinese cabbage, it is one of the most popular cabbages used in Asian cuisine. It has a very subtle and delicate flavor and may be eaten raw or used in a variety of ways: pickled to make kimchi, chopped and added to dumpling fillings, sautéed, or cooked in soups and stews.

15 Korean Watercress has a slightly bitter taste. It is considered an aquatic herb, but may also be used like a green vegetable. It may be added to soups, but the cooking time should be kept to a minimum.

16 香菇 有乾的及新鮮二種。乾香菇比新鮮香菇有香味,使用前需先泡軟。二者皆可用來炒、與肉燒煮、或加入湯內,新鮮香菇尚可用來烤食,須注意的是新鮮香菇烹飪時間要短,乾香菇則較耐煮。

17 魚乾 主要是用來熬高湯及增進菜餚的鮮味。魚高湯的做法,見 8 頁。

18 韓國梨 汁多、爽口且有特殊的芳香,有黃色及咖啡色兩種。除了當水果吃外,可與生牛肉或生魚拌食,也可切碎與其他調味品混合當沾料。

16 Shiitake mushrooms Also known as "Chinese black mushrooms," they are sold either fresh or dried. The dried ones have a stronger flavor than the fresh and are loved for their smoky and woody taste. Soak dried mushrooms in warm water (approx. 20 min) until soft then remove the stems before cooking. They are prepared in various ways: grilled, stewed, stir-fried, etc.

17 Dried anchovy A small, silvery salt-water fish, often used to make or enhance the flavor of a stock for soups, stews and sauces. Anchovy stock is described on p. 8.

18 Korean pear Also known as Japanese pear, Asian pear and apple pear, this juicy, crispy and aromatic fruit normally comes in yellow or brown skinned varieties. Not only enjoyed raw or made into sweet desserts, it can be added to all kinds of dishes, such as tartar, or made into sauces for noodle dishes.

常用調味料
SEASONINGS AND CONDIMENTS

1 麻油 炒芝麻碾壓製造而成濃郁香味的麻油,是韓國菜中重要的調味品。

2 海鹽 是由海水提煉出來的天然鹽,味道比一般鹽略淡,它能保持蔬菜爽脆及增進菜餚的風味,故韓國人在醃製泡菜或做其他菜餚時,喜歡使用海鹽。本書內所用的鹽皆為海鹽。

1 Sesame Oil The flavor is toasty, nutty and robust. It is pressed from roasted sesame seeds and is absolutely essential in Korean cuisine.

2 Sea salt A natural salt that is cultivated from sea water. Many Koreans prefer it over regular table salt because of its fresh, light taste. When pickling or making kimchi, sea salt is especially preferred, because it is known to help keep vegetables crisp. All measurements of salt in this book refer to the use of sea salt. Sea salt is lighter than regular salt. If regular salt is used, reduce the amount accordingly.

3 **牛肉精** 通常用來放入湯或其他菜餚內以增鮮味。其成份含濃縮牛肉湯、大蒜、洋蔥、大豆、鹽、黑胡椒、葡萄糖，偶爾也含味精。

蛤蜊精 適用於以海鮮材料為主的湯以增鮮味。其成份包含鹽、蛤蜊粉，偶爾也含玉米粉及味精。

4 **醬油** 以黃豆、小麥及鹽發酵製成。在書中除非有特別註明，否則均指一般醬油。

5 **韓國醬油** 此種醬油色淡味鹹，適用於色淺的菜餚或湯。.

6 **韓國辣椒粉** 將新鮮的紅辣椒烘乾後，磨成粗或細粉狀，韓國超市有售。在烹煮韓國菜或製作泡菜時經常使用，是做韓國菜的必備材料之一。微辣的辣椒粉，可使菜餚增添令人垂涎的鮮紅色澤。價格隨品質而差別，講究做菜的人，非常注重辣椒粉的選擇，另有一種"西班牙式紅椒粉"簡稱"西式紅椒粉"，色深紅較不辣，是用來加深菜餚的紅色。

7 **韓國辣椒醬** 由糯米、麵粉、辣椒粉、玉米糖漿及鹽製成，成份與中國的辣椒醬略不同但用途類似，是做韓國菜必備的辣醬。用來煮湯，也可與其他調味料混合當沾料或調味料使用。

3 **Beef bouillon (sogogi dashida)** A dry powder used mostly as a flavoring agent for soups, stews and sauces. It consists of beef extract, garlic, onion, soybean, salt, black pepper, glucose and occasionally MSG.

Clam bouillon (jogae dashida) Also comes as a dry powder, used mostly as a flavoring agent for seafood based soups, stews and sauces. It consists of salt, clam powder and occasionally, corn starch and MSG.

4 **Soy sauces** are fermented products of soybeans, wheat and salt. Unless specified, a regular soy sauce such as Kikkoman or Wei-Chuan soy sauce is used in this book.

5 **Korean soy sauce** *(kuk kang jang)* Lighter in color, but saltier in flavor than the above regular soy sauce. The Korean term, "kuk kang jang" literally means "soup soy sauce." It is used mostly for light color dishes and soups.

6 **Red pepper powder** *(go chu ga ru)* This book uses the spicier Korean style which is hotter than paprika. Derived from fresh red chillies, it is dried and ground into coarse or fine powder. An essential ingredient in Korean cuisine, it is used extensively and liberally in dishes. When added, the dish turns to a radiant, mouth watering red. The Koreans' love for spicy food is evident in the way red pepper powder is packaged and sold in the Korean markets: in huge sacks similar to the way rice or grain is packaged.

7 **Hot pepper paste** *(go chu jang)* There are many types of hot pepper paste used in most Asian cuisine. The Korean style hot pepper paste used in this book is a smooth and thick paste made from slowly cooking glutinous rice, flour, red pepper powder, corn syrup and salt. Another essential seasoning in a Korean pantry, it is added to meats, soups, stews, marinades, vegetable dressings, and also served as a spicy dip or hot relish.

8　豆瓣醬　由黃豆、糯米粉、麵粉及鹽製成，是韓國菜中重要調味料之一。與日本的"味噌"類似，可用來做湯，也可與其他調味料混合當沾料或調味料使用。不同品牌的豆瓣醬，顏色由淡黃色到深咖啡色皆有，每個人偏好不一，可選一種自己喜歡的或選二種不同的豆瓣醬混合使用。

9　味酥　以糯米釀製，色透明、味甜、有酒味。

10 米醋　本書內所使用的均為米醋，若無可用白醋取代。

11 濃縮醋　濃縮而成的醋非常酸。喜食酸味者，可隨喜好滴數滴在菜餚內。

12 玉米糖漿　從玉米煉製而成的甜味濃漿。

8　**Soybean paste *(den jang)*** An important item in a Korean pantry, it is primarily made from fermented soybeans, glutinous rice, wheat flour and salt. It is similar to the Japanese soy bean paste (*miso*), has a salty flavor and is used to make soups, stews, sauces, marinades, and dips. There are several varieties and brands of soybean paste in most Asian markets, ranging from mustard yellow to dark brown. As every chef has his or her preference, different types of paste may be combined in the same dish or used interchangeably.

9　**Mirin (sweet rice wine)** Another indispensible ingredient in Korean cuisine, it tastes sweet and is naturally brewed from glutinous rice.

10 **Rice vinegar** Used in many Asian cuisines, it has a clear to light golden color, with a delicate, subtly sweet flavor. If unavailable, distilled white vinegar may be substituted.

11 **Concentrated vinegar *(gang cho)*** A concentrated and pungent vinegar, it is used occasionally and sparingly, mostly as a fortifier or as an added zesty punch to a dish that calls for a strong vinegary taste.

12 **Corn syrup** Derived from corn kernels, it is used occassionally in Korean cooking. At times, it may be added to meat stews, crab, or vegetable side dishes.

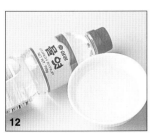

調味醬汁做法
PREPARING SPECIAL SAUCES

以下為韓國菜常使用的沾醬、沙拉醬、沾汁、烤醬及拌飯醬等。製作醬汁時可一次做多些，分數次享用。

The following sauces include salad dressings, dipping sauces, and other accompaniments. These sauces are often used to accessorize and intensify the flavors of the dish. Some sauces are very popular and more frequently used than others. Large portions may be made in advance and kept fresh in the refrigerator for more frequent use.

酸辣沾醬
SOUR & HOT SAUCE
(CHO GO CHU JANG)

韓國辣椒醬	1 杯
可樂、汽水或水	5 大匙
醋、橘子汁	各 5 大匙
糖、玉米糖漿	各 3 大匙
麻油	1 小匙
蒜、薑汁	各 ½ 小匙
紅酒	1 大匙

1 c. hot pepper paste (go-chu-jang)
5 T. cola, soda or water,
5 T. ea.: orange juice, vinegar
3 T. ea.: sugar, corn syrup
1 t. sesame oil
½ t. ea.: garlic juice, ginger juice
1 T. red wine

全部材料攪勻，即為大家喜愛的韓國沾醬，除用來作為前菜、生海鮮、蔬菜的沾料外，也可用來拌飯。

Mix all ingredients evenly. This is one of the most popular and versatile sauces used in Korean cuisine. It can be served with appetizers, steamed rice, raw seafood, cooked or fresh vegetables.

煎餅沾醬
PANCAKE SAUCE
(YANG NYUM JANG)

醬油	¼ 杯
洋蔥、蔥、紅甜椒、紅蘿蔔(全切碎)	各 1 小匙
糖、韓國辣椒粉、麻油	各 1 小匙
炒芝麻	½ 小匙

¼ c. soy sauce
1 t. ea.(minced): onion, green onion, red bell pepper, carrot
1 t. ea.: sugar, red pepper powder, sesame oil
½ t. toasted sesame seeds

全部材料放入果汁機內攪打成濃汁即成。可做為各種麵皮捲、煎餅、海鮮、肉及蔬菜的沾料。也可用來拌飯。

Mix all ingredients in blender thoroughly. This is a delicious go-with-anything sauce: pancakes, steamed rice, seafood, meat and vegetables.

韓式沙拉醬
ROMAINE SALAD DRESSING

淡色醬油	1 杯
麻油、檸檬汁	各 1 大匙
醋	⅓ 杯，糖 14 大匙
韓國辣椒粉	3 大匙
紅甜椒(切碎)	2 大匙
薑末	1 小匙
蒜末	1 小匙

1 c. soy sauce
1 T. ea.: sesame oil, lemon juice
⅓ c. vinegar, 14 T. sugar
3 T. red pepper powder
2 T. minced red bell pepper
1 t. minced ginger root
1 t. minced garlic clove

全部材料攪拌均勻，即成為沙拉醬，喜食酸味者可再加濃縮醋，拌好的蔬菜沙拉味濃可與飯配食。

Serve Romaine Salad, Korean style! Mix all the ingredients thoroughly. If a strong vinegary taste is preferred, add 1 t. of concentrated vinegar ("gangcho").

人蔘烤醬
SWEET GINSENG SOY SAUCE

糖、醬油	各 1 杯
水	1 ½ 杯
小柳丁(連皮切片)	½ 個
新鮮人蔘⋯1 片，薑	3 大片

1 c. ea: sugar, soy sauce
1 ½ c. water
½ unpeeled orange, sliced
1 ginseng root slice, 3 ginger slices

全部材料煮開後，改小火煮 2 小時，過濾後放置一夜；再煮開以玉米粉拌水勾芡成稀糊狀。用途與 "照燒醬" 同，可塗在雞、牛肉或茄子上烤。

Bring all ingredients to a boil, reduce to low heat and cook for 2 hours. Drain. Let stand overnight then reheat. To thicken, stir in a mixture of 1 1/2 T. cornstarch and 1 T. water. This sauce may be used like a terriyaki sauce, spreading it over charbroiled or BBQ meat.

醬油烤肉沾汁
BBQ DIPPING SAUCE

水	1 杯
辣椒(切段)	5 支
醬油、醋	各 5 大匙
糖⋯2 1/3 大匙，鹽	1 大匙
檸檬汁	2 大匙

1 c. water
5 jalapeño, chopped
5 T. ea.: soy sauce, vinegar
2 ⅛ T. sugar, 1 T. salt
2 T. lemon juice

全部材料放入果汁機內打碎，置冰箱 2-3 天再使用效果更佳。此沾汁是用來沾烤肉及鍋貼，也可做為煎魚的淋汁。

Mix all ingredients in the blender thoroughly. The flavor of this sauce may be further enriched after storing in the refrigerator for 2-3 days. This sauce goes with BBQ meat and can be used in fish dishes.

味噌沾醬
MIXED BEAN PASTE (SAM JANG)

日本白味噌	2 大匙
豆瓣醬	½ 小匙
韓國辣椒醬	½ 小匙
牛高湯 （見 8 頁）	3 大匙
糖、麻油	各 1 小匙
蒜末	½ 小匙

2 T. miso (Japanese white bean paste)
½ t. soybean paste (den-jang)
½ t. hot pepper paste (go-chu-jang)
3 T. beef stock (p.8)
1 t. ea.: sugar, sesame oil
½ t. minced garlic clove

將全部材料攪拌均勻。此醬是專用來塗在烤肉上，以生菜包捲而食。

Mix all ingredients thoroughly into a thick paste. Spread the sauce on the BBQ meat (pp.43-47) and wrap in lettuce leaves before serving.

菜飯辣醬
HOT SAUCE (BIBIMBAP SAUCE)

韓國辣椒醬	1 杯
可樂或水	3 大匙
牛高湯	2 大匙
紅酒、麻油、糖	各 1 大匙
西班牙式紅椒粉	1 小匙
蒜末	1/2 小匙

1 c. hot pepper paste (go-chu-jang)
3 T. cola or water
2 T. beef stock
1 T. ea.: red wine, sesame oil, sugar
1 t. paprika
½ t. minced garlic clove

將全部材料攪拌均勻成醬狀，此種醬適用於拌飯。

Mix all ingredients evenly into a paste. This spicy paste is used frequently to complement rice dishes.

蟹肉麵皮捲
DUNGENESS CRAB CREPES *(KE SAL MARI)*

餡：

① ┌ 熟蟹鉗肉 ....1 杯
　 └ 白胡椒 ....少許

② ┌ 蒜苗（或蔥白）...........切段 1 杯
　 └ 牛高湯（見 8 頁）.............1 杯

皮：

③ ┌ 菠菜葉 ....5 片
　 └ 水 ....½ 杯

④ ┌ 玉米粉 ....¼ 杯
　 └ 麵粉 ....¼ 杯

芥末沾醬：

⑤ ┌ 芥末粉 ....1 大匙
　 │ 糖 ....2 ½ 大匙
　 │ 美乃茲 ....3 大匙
　 │ 醋 ....7 大匙
　 └ 冰塊 ....3 塊

1 **餡** 將 ② 料煮開，改小火煮至蒜苗變軟，撈出待冷瀝乾水份，加 ① 料拌勻即成餡，分成 14 份。

2 **皮** 將 ③ 料放入果汁機內攪打後取出過濾，濾出的菠菜汁加 ④ 料拌勻即成綠色稀麵糊，若僅用水 ½ 杯加 ④ 料拌勻即成白色稀麵糊。

無油的不黏鍋內，一次一大匙將麵糊放入，把表面略抹一下成直徑 8 公分的薄皮，以小火煎至邊翹起即可取出。共做 14 張皮。

3 **芥末沾醬** 將 ⑤ 料放入果汁機內攪打成濃汁。

4 每張薄麵皮上，各放入一份蟹餡，捲成圓筒狀（也可用油 1 小匙，以中火煎至表面微焦），沾"芥末沾醬"食用。

什錦麵皮捲

將上面蟹肉餡改為什錦餡。香菇、筍、紅蘿蔔、黃瓜絲共 1½ 杯一起炒好，牛肉、蝦仁、罐頭鮑魚絲共 1 杯也一起炒好，蛋 1 個煎成蛋皮切絲，全部材料略加鹽、胡椒拌勻即成。其他材料及做法同上。

Filling:

① ┌ 1 c. cooked Dungeness
　 │　　crab meat, shredded
　 └ pinch of white pepper

② ┌ 1 c. leek or white part of
　 │　　green onions, sectioned
　 └ 1 c. beef broth (p.8)

Crepes:

③ ┌ 5 spinach leaves
　 └ ½ c. water

④ ┌ ¼ c. cornstarch
　 └ ¼ c. all-purpose flour

Mustard sauce :

⑤ ┌ 1 T. Coleman dry mustard
　 │ 2 ½ T. sugar
　 │ 3 T. mayonnaise
　 │ 7 T. vinegar
　 └ 3 ice cubes

1 **Filling** Boil ②, then turn heat to low; cook until leek turns soft. Remove, drain and let cool. Mix leek with ① then divide into 14 portions.

2 **Crepes** Mix ③ in a blender then strain. Mix the strained spinach juice with ④ to form a thin green batter. If ④ is mixed with ½ c. water instead of pureed ③, it will make a white batter.

Put 1 T. batter into a non-stick pan. Swirl the pan to form a 3" (8cm) diameter thin crepe. Use low heat to fry the crepe untill the edges curl. Repeat and make a total of 14 crepes.

3 **Mustard sauce** Mix ⑤ in a blender until it becomes a thick sauce.

4 Place dungeness crab filling on each crepe, then roll up in a cone shape. (Crepes may be fried with 1 t. oil, at medium heat, until the surface turns slightly golden). Serve with mustard sauce.

ROYAL PLATE *(KU JUL PAN)*

Replace the above filling with the following ingredients: Shredded shiitake mushrooms, bamboo shoots, carrots and cucumber to equal 1½ c. then stir-fry. Shred beef, shrimp, and canned abalone to equal 1c. then stir-fry. Pan-fry one beaten egg, then shred. Combine all of these ingredients, toss and add salt and pepper to taste. Follow the above recipe's procedures to make the crepes, then add the Royal Plate filling.

鑲蛤蜊
BROILED GIANT CLAM *(DAE HAP GUI)*

白色魚餅.................切丁 ¼ 杯
象拔蚌肉、洋菇....切丁各 ½ 杯
鹽.........................¼ 小匙
黑胡椒......................少許
① ┌ 蝦仁......½ 杯，鹽...½ 小匙
   └ 白胡椒...................少許
濃奶精 * ....1 杯
蛤蜊殼(大) ....4 個

¼ c. diced white fish cake
½ c. ea.(diced): giant clam,
   mushrooms
¼ t. salt
pinch of black pepper
① ┌ ½ c. shelled shrimp
   │ ½ t. salt
   └ pinch of white pepper
1 c. heavy cream
4 large cherry stone clam
   shells

1 油 1 小匙燒熱，將魚餅略炒，續入象拔蚌炒至肉變白，再入洋菇、鹽及黑胡椒略炒鏟出。

2 將 ① 料放入攪碎機切碎，再加入濃奶精，攪勻成濃漿，取出與炒好的材料拌勻後分成 4 份，逐個鑲入蛤蜊殼內。

3 水燒開，鑲好的蛤蜊置蒸盤，以大火蒸 7 分鐘至熟即可，食前放入烤箱，用最高溫(broil)至表面呈金黃色，盤底以海鹽當盤飾，是為一道精美的前菜。

★ 濃奶精比一般加入咖啡內的奶精濃，通常使用在濃湯內。

1 Heat 1 t. oil, briefly fry white fish cake, add diced giant clam and stir-fry until the clam meat turns white. Add mushrooms, salt and pepper. Set aside.

2 Blend ① in a food processor, add heavy cream and blend again into a mousse. Mix with the above stir-fried ingredients, then divide into 4 portions. Place the filling into each individual shell.

3 Bring water to a boil, steam the filled clam shells in a steamer over high heat for 7 minutes or until cooked. Use high heat to bake until the top turns golden brown, then serve. Place sea salt on the bottom of the shells as a garnish. This is a very delightful appetizer.

鑲茄子
BROILED EGGPLANT *(GAJI GUI)*

茄子.........................2 條
① 料同上
濃奶精 * ....1 杯
人參烤醬 (見 17 頁) ......1 大匙

2 eggplants
① same as above recipe
1 c. heavy cream
1 T. sweet ginseng soy sauce
   (p.17)

1 茄子對切二，由皮面上挖出茄肉(圖 1)，以便鑲餡。

2 將 ① 料放入攪碎機切碎，再入濃奶精，攪成濃漿，分成四份，逐個鑲入茄子內。

3 水燒開，茄子置蒸盤內，以大火蒸約 5 分鐘至餡料熟，茄子變軟即可。

4 食前淋上 "人參烤醬" 後放入烤箱用最高溫(broil)烤至表面成金黃色。

★ 濃奶精比一般加入咖啡內的奶精濃，通常使用在濃湯內。

1 Cut each eggplant in half. Slice each previously cut half lengthwise again to remove the curved portion from the half (Fig.1). Remove a portion of the flesh from the remaining eggplant, creating a concave shape.

2 Blend ① in a food processor, add heavy cream and blend again into a mousse. Divide into 4 portions, then fill into each eggplant.

3 Bring water to a boil, place stuffed eggplants in the steamer. Use high heat to steam for 5 minutes until soft.

4 Spread ginseng soy sauce on the eggplants and put in oven and broil until the surface turns to a beautiful golden brown; serve.

甜 酸 辣 雞 翅
SPICY CHICKEN WINGS (*DAK NAL KE JO RIM*)

雞翅 10 隻......1 斤(600 公克)

① ┌ 胡椒 ....¼ 小匙
│ 鹽、蒜末...............各 ½ 小匙
│ 洋蔥末 ....1 大匙
└ 蛋白 ....1 個

麵粉 ....2 大匙
炸油 ....適量

② ┌ 糖、韓國辣椒醬 ......各 1 大匙
│ 米醋 ....4 大匙
│ 酸辣汁(Tabasco) ....2 大匙
│ 蜂蜜、醬油 ....各 2 大匙
└ 韓國辣椒粉、蒜末..各 ½ 小匙

1 為易於食用，雞翅在細小的一端順週圍切一圈，再直劃一刀，以便把皮連肉向粗的一端翻下(圖 1)成"棒棒糖"狀。

2 將雞翅拌入 ① 料略醃，直立放入蒸盤，蓋上保鮮膜(圖 2)，水燒開用大火蒸 10 分鐘至熟，取出沾上麵粉。

3 炸油燒熱，放入雞翅炸至外皮酥脆撈出。

4 將 ② 料拌勻燒開，煮至略稠放入雞翅拌勻盛出，此菜非常可口可當主菜或前菜。

■ **盤飾** 醬油、糖、蒜及水煮開後，放入燙熟的蔥略拌即撈出，不僅可食，也可當盤飾。

10 chicken wings, 1 ⅓ lbs. (600g)

① ┌ ¼ t. pepper
│ ½ t. ea.: salt, minced garlic clove
│ 1 T. minced onion
└ 1 egg white

2 T. all-purpose flour
oil for deep-frying

② ┌ 1 T. ea.: sugar, hot pepper paste (go chu jang)
│ 4 T. rice vinegar
│ 2 T. tabasco sauce
│ 2 T. ea.: honey, soy sauce
└ ½ t. ea.: red pepper powder, minced garlic clove

1 Cut around the narrow side of the chicken wings, then cut lengthwise in order for the skin and meat to be folded downward (Fig.1) like a "lollipop".

2 Marinate chicken wings in ①. Place vertically in a steamer, then cover with plastic wrap (Fig.2). Boil water, steam the chicken wings over high heat for 10 minutes until cooked. Remove and coat with flour.

3 Heat oil for deep-frying, deep-fry chicken wings until crispy. Remove.

4 Bring mixed ② to a boil, cook and stir over high heat until thickened. Put in chicken wings and mix well. This recipe combines sweet, sour and spicy flavors and can be served as an entree or appetizer.

■ **Garnishes** Blanch green onions; drain. Heat soy sauce, sugar, garlic and water in a small sauce pan. Bring to a boil, add green onions until lightly coated with sauce. Remove and decorate. It's a delight to the palate.

海鮮煎餅
SEAFOOD PANCAKES (PA JUN)

① 魷魚、青椒.........切絲各 ¼ 杯
　　蝦仁(小) ....¼ 杯
　　大紅椒絲 ....1 大匙
　　蔥段 ....2 杯

② 糯米粉、麵粉 ....各 ¼ 杯
　　白胡椒 ....少許
　　鹽、蒜末、麻油 .....各 ¼ 小匙

③ 蛋(打散).........................1 個
　　水 ....2 大匙

煎餅沾醬(見 16 頁).........適量

1 將 ② 料盛於盆內，分次加入拌勻的 ③ 料攪勻（圖 1），再加 ① 料(圖 2)即成海鮮麵糊。

2 油 1 大匙燒熱，放入麵糊壓成 1 大片，煎成兩面金黃色至熟，表面酥脆即盛出，沾"煎餅沾醬"食用。

■ 這是特殊場合頗受歡迎的傳統菜，除當前菜外，也可當點心。煎餅一般不放豬、牛、或雞等肉類，但任何海鮮或蔬菜均可加入予以變化。

① ¼ c. ea.(shredded): squid, green bell pepper
　¼ c. shelled small shrimp
　1 T. shredded red bell pepper
　2 c. sectioned green onions

② ¼ c. ea.: sweet rice flour, all-purpose flour
　pinch of white pepper
　¼ t. ea.: salt, minced garlic clove, sesame oil

③ 1 egg. beaten
　2 T. water

pancake sauce (p.16) as desired

1 Put ② in a bowl, pour in ③ slowly and mix (Fig.1); add ① (Fig.2) and stir to make a seafood batter.

2 Heat 1 T. oil; pour in seafood batter to form large pancake. Fry until both sides are golden and crispy. Serve with pancake sauce.

■ This is a popular traditional dish often served during special occasions. It also makes an excellent appetizer or snack. Variations of this dish can be made by replacing seafood with mixed vegetables. Almost any kind of seafood or vegetables may be used in ①. However, pork, beef and chicken are not suitable for this dish.

綠豆餅
MUNG BEAN PANCAKES *(BIN DAE DUK)*

去皮綠豆 * ....1 杯
1 ⌈ 韓國泡菜 ....⅓ 杯
  ⌊ 綠豆芽 ....2 大匙
2 ⌈ 鹽、麻油 ....各 1 小匙
  | 大紅椒(切碎) ....1 小匙
  ⌊ 白胡椒、蒜末 ....各少許
煎餅沾醬(見 16 頁) ....適量

1 c. skinless mung beans*
1 ⌈ **⅓ c. Korean kimchi**
  ⌊ **2 T. mung bean sprouts**
2 ⌈ **1 t. ea.: salt, sesame oil**
  | **1 t. minced red bell pepper**
  | **pinch of white pepper**
  | **minced garlic cloves as**
  | **desired**
  ⌊ **pancake sauce (p.16) as**
     desired

1 綠豆沖洗去砂石,再用水 1¼ 杯浸泡 2 小時以上,放入果汁機內打成泥狀。

2 將 1 料洗淨擠乾並切碎,連同綠豆泥及 2 料拌勻,做成 10 個直徑 5 公分的圓餅。

3 油 1 大匙燒熱,用中火將餅煎成金黃色,食時沾醬油或"煎餅沾醬"。

★ 已去皮綠豆超市有售。

■ 餅上貼些綠葉及紅甜椒等,煎出來的餅格外出色,在韓國、日本及洛杉磯非常受歡迎。

1 Rinse mung beans with water to remove sand and stones. Refill with 1 1/4 c. water and let soak for more than 2 hours. Put beans and water in blender and blend to a fine mash.

2 Wash 1, squeeze out water; then mince. Add mung beans, and 2; mix well. Divide and make into 10 flat circular pancakes, each 2" (5 cm) in diameter.

3 Heat 1 T. oil; fry pancakes over medium heat until golden brown. Serve with soy sauce or pancake sauce.

★ Skinless mung beans are avaiable in Asian markets.

■ May add green leaf or red bell pepper to enhance and beautify presentation. This is a popular dish in Korea, Japan and Los Angeles.

紫蘇干貝夾
SCALLOPS IN OBA LEAVES *(SCALLOPS TI KIM)*

干貝 4 塊 ....¼ 杯
炸粉 ....⅓ 杯
紫蘇葉 ....8 片
1 ⌈ 麵包粉 ....¼ 杯
  ⌊ 韓國西洋菜(或香菜)..切碎 ¼ 杯
炸油 ....適量
酸辣沾醬(見 16 頁) ....適量

4 scallops (¼ c.)
⅓ c. frying mix
8 oba leaves
1 ⌈ **¼ c. fine bread crumbs**
  | **¼ c. minced Korean**
  | **watercress or minced**
  ⌊   **coriander**
oil for deep-frying
sour & hot sauce (p.16) as
   desired

1 干貝在滾水內川燙撈出。炸粉加 ¼ 杯的水拌成麵糊,1 料拌勻備用。

2 每片紫蘇葉沾麵糊後在其兩面略撒些 1 料(不要太多),干貝置葉上並加"酸辣沾醬"½ 小匙(圖 1),再蓋上另一片紫蘇葉,兩葉週圍用麵糊黏住即成紫蘇干貝夾。

3 炸油燒熱,中火將干貝夾炸至酥脆,放在"炸馬鈴薯圈"上。

■ **炸馬鈴薯圈** 小馬鈴薯去皮修成圓柱形後,繞表面切 1-2 圈薄片,用油炸酥。

1 Blanch scallops in boiling water. Combine frying mix with ¼ c. water to form a batter. Mix 1 and set aside.

2 Coat each oba leaf in batter and sprinkle 1 on both sides lightly. Place a scallop on an oba leaf, add ½ t. of sour & hot sauce (Fig.1), and cover with another oba leaf. Seal around outer edge of leaf with batter.

3 Heat oil for deep-frying; fry filled oba leaf over medium heat until crispy. Place on a "fried potato slice."

■ **Fried potato slice** Using a small potato, remove rounded ends. Cut around the potato so the center now forms a cylinder. Hold a cutting knife parallel to the cylinder and cut a long continuous circular slice around the potato one or two turns. Deep-fry until crispy.

鑲青椒
STUFFED CHILI PEPPERS (GO CHU JUN)

韓國辣椒 * ....10 條
① ┌ 牛絞肉 ....1 杯
 └ 豆腐(壓碎擠乾) ....¼ 杯
② ┌ 醬油 ....½ 小匙
 │ 麻油 ....½ 小匙
 │ 鹽 ....1 小匙
 │ 糖 ....2 小匙
 │ 胡椒 ....¼ 小匙
 │ 炒芝麻 ....1 小匙
 │ 蔥末 ....¼ 杯
 └ 蒜末 ....½ 小匙
 麵粉 ....1 小匙
 蛋(打散) ....1 個
 煎餅沾醬(見 16 頁)........適量

1 辣椒(圖 1)對切成兩半,去籽拭乾。

2 將 ① 料拌入 ② 料用力攪至有黏性即為餡。

3 每片辣椒內撒上麵粉,再沾蛋汁(圖 2),鑲入肉餡。

4 油 1 大匙燒熱,肉面朝下,煎至肉熟,表面呈金黃色。食時可沾醬油或"煎餅沾醬"。

★ 韓國辣椒略帶辣味,挑選約 12 公分長,皮薄且嫩的為佳,否則需先略蒸一下軟化再用。

---

10 Korean chili peppers*
① ┌ **1 c. ground beef**
 └ **¼ c. tofu (crushed and pressed dry)**
② ┌ **½ t. soy sauce**
 │ **½ t. sesame oil**
 │ **1 t. salt**
 │ **2 t. sugar**
 │ **¼ t. pepper**
 │ **1 t. toasted sesame seeds**
 │ **¼ c. minced green onions**
 └ **½ t. minced garlic clove**
 1 t. all-purpose flour
 1 egg, beaten
 pancake sauce (p.16) as desired

1 Cut peppers (Fig.1) in half, lengthwise; remove seeds. Pat dry.

2 Mix ① with ② thoroughly until sticky to create filling.

3 Sprinkle flour on both sides, then dip in beaten egg (Fig.2), place filling in each half.

4 Heat 1 T. oil, pan-fry pepper filling side down. Fry until fillings are cooked and surfaces are golden brown. Serve with soy sauce or pancake sauce.

★ Korean chili peppers are slightly spicy. Select peppers that are 5" (12 cm) long with delicate and tender skin. If the pepper used is not tender, steam before use.

上湯水餃
DUMPLING SOUP *(MAN DU KOOK)*

1 上湯水餃 將牛高湯(見 8 頁)5 杯燒開，放入下面做好的 "泡菜水餃" 20 個煮至熟，可隨意加蔥絲，燒滾後分盛於 2 只碗內，上撒紫菜絲即可。

1 Boil 5 c. beef broth (p.8), then add 20 kimchi dumplings from the recipe below, boil until cooked. Add shredded green onions as desired. Bring to boil, then separate in 2 bowls, sprinkle some seaweed (kim) on top; serve.

泡菜水餃
KIMCHI DUMPLINGS *(KIMCHI MANDO)*

1
- 牛絞肉 ....½ 杯
- 泡菜(切碎).......................1½ 杯
- 豆腐(壓碎)........................¼ 杯
- 綠豆芽、熟冬粉 * ..切碎各 ¼ 杯

2
- 麻油 ....2 小匙
- 味醂、鹽................各 ½ 小匙
- 黑胡椒 ....少許

水餃皮 ....20 張
炸油 ....適量
醬油烤肉沾汁(見 17 頁).....適量

1
- ½ c. ground beef
- 1½ c. minced kimchi
- ¼ c. mashed tofu
- ¼ c. ea. (minced): mung bean sprouts, cooked glass noodles*

2
- 2 t. sesame oil
- ½ t. ea.: mirin, salt
- pinch of black pepper

20 sheets dumpling skin
oil for deep-frying
BBQ dipping sauce (p.17) as desired

1 將 1 及 2 料拌勻成餡分 20 份。每張水餃皮內放入 1 份餡(圖 1)，皮的邊緣沾水折半，一面皮打摺(圖 2)，包成餃子狀(圖 3)。

2 炸油燒熱，將水餃放入，炸至餡熟、表面微焦，沾 "醬油烤肉沾汁" 食用。

* 將水燒滾後熄火，再把冬粉 1 小包，1.5 兩(56 公克)泡 5 分鐘後撈出，再用清水漂涼瀝乾可得 1 杯。

■ 做好的水餃可煎、蒸或水煮。

1 Mix 1 and 2 to make filling; divide into 20 portions. Place one filling in the center of each dumpling skin (Fig.1). Moisten edges of skins with water. Fold over in half and pleat one side of dumpling skin (Fig.2); lightly press edges together to seal (Fig.3).

2 Heat oil for deep-frying; fry dumplings until filling is cooked and skin is brown. Serve with BBQ dipping sauce.

* Boil water, then turn off heat, add 2 oz. (56g) glass noodles and soak for 5 minutes until soft; remove. Rinse with clean water and drain, resulting in 1 c.

■ Dumplings may be served pan-fried, steamed, or boiled.

魚片燒賣
FISH DUMPLINGS (AW MANDU)

牛高湯(見 8 頁)或水.........2 杯
1 ┌ 高麗菜(切絲).....................2 杯
  └ 蔥白(切粗粒).....................1 杯
2 ┌ 新鮮香菇(切條)................3 朵
  └ 大紅椒(切條)................1 大匙
3 ┌ 鹽.............................1 小匙
  └ 白胡椒.......................¼ 小匙
蝦仁(剁爛) ....½ 杯
小蝦(留尾)....................4 隻
魚片(12×12 公分薄片)....4 張
鋁紙(12×12 公分薄片).....4 張

1 牛高湯燒開，將 1 料依序放入，煮至軟撈出擠乾水份。

2 油 1 小匙燒熱，先炒煮過的 1 料再入 2 及 3 料略炒盛出待冷後，加剁爛的蝦泥拌成餡料分成 4 份。

3 鋁紙 1 張塗上一層油，上置魚片，放入 1 份餡中間插入 1 隻蝦，用魚片包住餡料露出蝦尾(圖 1)，再用鋁紙包住，以固定形狀。

4 水燒開，蒸盤內放入鋁紙包，大火蒸 10 分鐘取出，去除鋁紙，隨意用燙熟的細蔥綁住蝦尾當裝飾。

■ 此精美的菜餚，適合宴客時做為前菜。

2 c. beef broth (p.8) or water
1 ┌ **2 c. shredded cabbage**
  │ **1 c. chopped white part of**
  └ **green onions**
2 ┌ **3 shiitake mushrooms, cut**
  │ **in strips**
  │ **1 T. red bell peppers, cut in**
  └ **strips**
3 ┌ **1 t. salt**
  └ **¼ t. white pepper**
½ c. shelled shrimp,
minced
4 small shelled shrimp with
tails intact
4 thin fish slices, 5"×5"
(12×12cm)
4 sheets aluminum foil, 5"×
5" (12×12cm)

1 Boil beef broth, add 1 in the order listed. Cook until vegetables are soft. Drain and squeeze out water.

2 Heat 1 t. oil. Stir-fry 1, add 2 and 3, mix well and stir-fry briefly. Remove and let cool. Mix with minced shrimp. Divide into four equal portions.

3 Brush oil on aluminum foil. Place a fish slice on foil, then add one portion of filling on top of fish, insert one shrimp into top of filling. Fold fish slice over the filling, leaving the shrimp tail exposed (Fig.1). Fold over foil to keep the shape. Repeat the remaining portions.

4 Boil water. Place dumplings in steamer over high heat for ten minutes. Remove foil, tie pre-cooked green onion strips around shrimp tails as garnish.

■ A favorite banquet appetizer enjoyed for its elegant presentation.

1

辣味燒豆腐
SPICY BRAISED TOFU *(DU BU JO RIM)*

豆腐..............12 兩(450 公克)

① ┌ 洋蔥..1 片
　 └ 蔥段..⅓ 杯

② ┌ 韓國醬油........................2 大匙
　 │ 韓國辣椒粉、醬油、麻油
　 │ ....各 1 小匙
　 │ 糖..1 大匙
　 │ 蒜末..½ 小匙
　 └ 魚高湯(見 8 頁)或水........2 杯

1 豆腐切成八片，修成一公分厚直徑 5 公分的圓片(圖 1)。

2 油 1 大匙燒熱，將豆腐煎成二面金黃色。

3 小鍋內置 ① 料再放入豆腐及 ② 料，燒開改中火，煮至汁略收乾，豆腐盛於盤內淋上餘汁。用炸餛飩皮、蓮藕及細蔥當盤飾。

煎豆腐
將豆腐切塊或切片後，二面煎黃，淋或沾"煎餅沾醬"(見 16 頁)。

1 lb. (450g), tofu

① ┌ 1 onion slice
　 └ ⅓ c. sectioned green
　 　 onions

② ┌ 2 T. Korean soy sauce (kuk
　 │ 　 kang jang)
　 │ 1 t. ea.: red pepper powder,
　 │ 　 soy sauce, sesame oil
　 │ 1 T. sugar
　 │ ½ t. minced garlic clove
　 │ 2 c. anchovy stock (p.8) or
　 └ 　 water

1 Cut tofu into eight square pieces; trim corners to form circles 2" (5cm) in diameter (Fig.1).

2 Heat 1 T. oil, fry each side of tofu until golden brown.

3 In a sauce pan, add ①, tofu and ②; when boiling, reduce heat to medium. Cook until sauce is almost evaporated. Place tofu on plate and pour the sauce over it. Use fried wanton skin, lotus root and green onion as garnish.

PAN-FRIED TOFU *(DU BU BUCHIM)*
Cut tofu as desired and pan-fry until both sides are golden brown. Serve with pancake sauce (p.16).

大麥紅綢魚
SEA BREAM WITH BARLEY *(DO MI BO RI SU DAN)*

紅綢魚 ....1 斤(600 公克)
1「鹽、胡椒 ....各 ¼ 小匙
　醬油烤肉沾汁(見 17 頁)
2 ....2 大匙
　└韓國辣椒粉 ....½ 小匙
　煮熟麥角 * ....⅓ 杯
　「蠔菇(略撕開) ....1 杯
　蔥段 ....1 杯
3 金針菇(切半) ....¼ 杯
　新鮮香菇(切塊) ....2 朵
　└紅蘿蔔絲 ....2 大匙
　「醬油 ....2 小匙
4 麻油 ....½ 小匙
　└糖 ....1 小匙

1 魚切除魚頭及魚骨，取出帶皮的魚肉 2 片(圖
　1)每片各 6 兩(225 公克)撒上 1 料。 2 料調
　勻備用。

2 油 1 小匙燒熱，放入 3 料略炒，再加入麥角
　及 4 料炒拌均勻盛盤。

3 油 1 大匙燒熱，先將魚皮面朝下，煎至二面呈
　金黃色後，入 2 料迅速翻面，置於炒好的蔬
　菜上，當前菜外也可當主菜與飯配食。

* 麥角先在多量水內煮熟後，撈出沾滾玉米粉，
　再放入篩內以滾水川燙撈出，反覆三次即成
　(圖 2)。

---

1 ⅓ lbs. (600g) sea bream
1 ⌈ ¼ t. ea.: salt, pepper
　2 T. BBQ dipping sauce
2 　(p.17)
　└ ½ t. red pepper powder
　⅓ c. cooked barley*
　⌈ 1 c. oyster mushrooms
　　(slightly shredded)
　1 c. sectioned green onions
　¼ c. enoki mushrooms, cut
3 　in half
　2 shiitake mushrooms, cut
　　in pieces
　└ 2 T. shredded carrot
　⌈ 2 t. soy sauce
4 ½ t. sesame oil
　└ 1 t. sugar

1 Cut off head and fillet fish into two pieces,
　leave skin on (Fig.1) each equaling 1/2 lb.
　(225g). Sprinkle on 1. Mix 2 and set aside.

2 Heat 1 t. oil. Lightly stir-fry 3, add barley and
　4. Mix well while stir-frying. Remove and put
　on a plate.

3 Heat 1 T. oil; pan-fry fish, skin side down
　initially. Flip fish and fry until golden brown on
　both sides. Add 2, quickly turn over and place
　atop the vegetables. This is a fine appetizer,
　or can be served with rice as a main dish.

* Barley is cooked in a large amount of boiling
　water until done. Drain and coat with
　cornstarch; put in a sifter and then blanch
　briefly in boiling water and drain again. Repeat
　this procedure three times (Fig.2).

素炒冬粉

GLASS NOODLES WITH VEGETABLES *(CHAP CHE)*

1 高麗菜、紅蘿蔔、洋蔥、蔥、
大紅椒、木耳（泡軟）..............
..............切絲共 6 兩(225 公克)
蒜末..........................¼ 小匙
熟冬粉 *..........................2 杯
2 醬油....2 大匙，黑胡椒..¼ 小匙
麻油、糖....................各 1 大匙

1 油 2 大匙燒熱，將蒜末炒香，先放入 ① 料略
炒再加冬粉翻拌，最後加入 ② 料炒拌均勻即
可。

* 將水燒滾後熄火，再把冬粉 2 小包，共 3 兩
(115 公克)泡 5 分鐘後撈出，再用清水漂涼瀝
乾可得 2 杯。

■ 此道菜是一般家庭及韓國餐館常見的家常菜。

1 ½ lb. (225g) total(shredded):
cabbage, carrot, onion, red
bell pepper, soaked dried
wood ears, green onion
¼ t. minced garlic clove
2 c. cooked glass noodles*
2 2 T. soy sauce, ¼ t. black
pepper
1 T. ea.: sesame oil, sugar

1 Heat 2 T. oil. Stir-fry garlic until fragrant. Add
① and lightly stir-fry; add glass noodles and
toss. Add mixture ② and mix well. Serve.

* Boil water, then turn off heat, add ¼ lb. (115g)
glass noodles and soak for 5 minutes until
soft; remove. Rinse with clean water and
drain, resulting in 2 c.

■ This is a very popular home style dish. It may
also be found in many restaurants in Korea.

辣炒鱆魚

SPICY OCTOPUS *(NAK JI BOK GUM)*

鱆魚 *..............6 兩(225 公克)
1 蒜末 ....½ 小匙
韓國辣椒醬....................2 大匙
2 辣椒、洋蔥、紅蘿蔔切片共 1½ 杯
3 味醂 ....½ 小匙
糖.......2 小匙，黑胡椒 ....少許
4 炒芝麻(壓碎)..1 大匙，蔥...4 段

1 鱆魚切成 5 公分長備用(圖 1)。

2 麻油 1 大匙燒熱，依序放入 ① 、 ② 料炒香，
再入鱆魚略炒至熟，再加 ③ 及 ④ 料續以大火
炒拌均勻。可與飯配食。

* 可用魷魚取代鱆魚。

½ lb. (225g) octopus*
½ t. minced garlic clove
1 2 T. hot pepper paste (go chu
jang)
2 1 ½ c. total (sliced):
jalapenos, onions, carrots
3 ½ t. mirin, 2 t. sugar
pinch of black pepper
4 1 T. toasted sesame seeds
(mashed)
4 green onion sections

1 Cut octopus into 2" (5cm) long pieces. Set
aside (Fig.1).

2 Heat 1 T. sesame oil. Stir-fry in order ① and ②
until fragrant. Add octopus and stir-fry until
cooked. Then add ③ and ④. Continue to cook
over high heat, stirring and mixing well. Serve
with rice.

* May substitute squid for octopus.

韓式生魚
TUNA TARTAR *(CHAM CHI HWE)*

鮪魚.................6 兩 (225 克)
韓國梨(或蘋果).............½ 個
⅟1 糖.................................1 大匙
醬油..............................¼ 小匙
檸檬汁..........................1 小匙
蒜汁、麻油................⅛ 小匙

1　鮪魚切絲(圖 1)冰涼，梨子去皮切絲，泡鹽水
　　以免變色，撈出備用。

2　食用時盤內先舖梨絲，鮪魚拌入 ⅟1 料舖在其
　　上。

½ lb. (225g) tuna
½ Korean pear or apple
⅟1 1 T. sugar
¼ t. soy sauce
1 t. lemon juice
⅛ t. ea.: garlic juice,
　　sesame oil

1　Shred tuna (Fig.1) and refrigerate. Peel pear
　　and shred; soak in salt water to preserve color,
　　then drain.

2　To serve, place shredded pear on a plate with
　　mixture of tuna and ⅟1 on top.

生拌牛肉
BEEF TARTAR *(YUK HWE)*

肋眼牛肉....... 6 兩(225 公克)
韓國梨(或蘋果)............. ½ 個
⅟1 醬油.............................. 1 大匙
糖................................1⅓ 大匙
黑胡椒..........................少許
⅟2 麻油.............................. 2 大匙
炒芝麻、蒜末..........各 1 小匙

1　牛肉切絲(牛肉先稍冰凍較容易切) (圖 2)，梨
　　子去皮切絲，泡鹽水以免變色，撈出備用。

2　食時盤內先舖梨絲，再將牛肉拌入 ⅟1 及 ⅟2 料
　　後，舖在梨絲上，可放生的鵪鶉蛋。

■　此菜類似歐洲的韃靼生牛排。

½ lb (225g) rib eye or lean
　　beef
½ Korean pear or apple
⅟1 1 T. soy sauce
1 ⅓ T. sugar
pinch of black pepper
⅟2 2 T. sesame oil
1 t. ea.: toasted sesame
　　seeds, minced garlic
　　cloves

1　Shred meat (Beef that is slightly frozen can be
　　shredded more easily)(Fig.2). Peel and shred
　　pear, soak in salt water to preserve color, then
　　drain.

2　To serve, place shredded pear on a plate with
　　mixture of beef, ⅟1 and ⅟2 on top. May put
　　uncooked quail egg on top.

■　This dish is similar to Steak Tartar, renowned
　　in European restaurants.

韓國燒烤
KOREAN BARBEQUE

提到韓國菜，很自然地會讓人想到美味的韓國燒烤。而韓國燒烤之所以別具特色，主要是有其獨特的醃料及在桌上烤食，四溢的香味，不僅令人垂涎三尺，更可讓您和家人、朋友一起享受邊烤邊食的樂趣。

醃肉要領 醬油、麻油、糖及蒜是主要調味料，利用辣豆瓣醬、薑末、胡椒及果汁等也可變化味道，必要時可加些切碎的奇異果泥及洋蔥泥增加肉的嫩度。 醃肉秘訣在於用手抓拌，使味道均勻地醃入肉內。

餐桌上的準備 在家中或餐廳裡，以小型的烤爐在室內桌上燒烤（見 9 頁），讓用餐者圍坐四周，便於即烤即食。燒烤時可準備白飯、湯、數種小菜、一些冰涼爽口的泡菜以及"醬油烤肉沾汁"（見 17 頁）。燒烤餐可豐富也可簡單；較豐盛的餐局可準備多種不同的蔬菜，如香菇、青、紅甜椒、南瓜、洋蔥等一起烤食，或另加前菜、飯後甜點等。

烹調的應用 醃肉時若大量醃製，除可分數次烤食外，亦可將已醃好的肉，用不黏鍋來烹煮，因醃料內加有麻油，故只需在燒熱的不黏鍋以大火炒至熟，不需另外再加油，對忙碌的上班族或家庭主婦非常方便。不論炒或烤，只要試過後絕對讓您回味無窮。

Anyone remotely familiar with Korean cuisine will have heard about the absolutely delicious Korean Barbeque. Meat or vegetables are first marinated, then grilled over a table-top burner. Eating as you barbeque is not only fun but also a very communal experience shared amongst families and friends. The aroma of the sizzling barbeque is guaranteed to make your mouth water. The anticipation is as much a part of the enjoyment as the immediate pleasure in eating the food as it's cooked.

Marinating Soy sauce, sesame oil, sugar and garlic are indispensible in the marinades; hot pepper paste, minced ginger, pepper and fruit juices are added for variation. When neccessary, finely minced kiwi and onions are used occasionally to tenderize the meat. Often times, the meat is rubbed and massaged by hand to ensure that the marinade is fully absorbed.

Table Setting and Barbequing In homes and restaurants, compact and portable table top burners with metal grids are used to barbeque foods indoors (p.9). The burner is set in the middle of the table and everyone circles around it, cooking and eating the sizzling barbeque right off the grill. The meal is usually accompanied by seasoned sauces, steamed rice, soup, a wide array of side dishes, and some cool and crunchy spicy kimchi for contrasting tastes. For a more elaborate meal, appetizers and sweet desserts, or extra vegetables such as shiitake mushrooms, bell peppers, squash, and onions may be added to the barbeque.

Other Cooking Methods For convenience, large quantities of meat may be marinated, then cooked and served throughout the week. The use of a non-stick frying pan is a great alternative for cooking the marinated foods. Since there is plenty of sesame oil in the marinade, it is unneccesary to add oil to the frying pan. The key is to keep the frying pan piping hot before frying. Whether it is stir-fried or barbequed, once you try it, you will desire it many times more.

烤肉的吃法

烤肉一般是沾"醬油烤肉沾汁"
或"味噌沾醬"（見 17 頁）食用。
若與"味噌沾醬"食用，則拿一片生菜，
把烤好的肉置於其上，再隨意加上
米飯、蒜片或泡菜包食。

Serving Methods

Take a lettuce leaf and wrap barbecued
meat with a bit of rice, thinly sliced garlic,
or some kimchi with mixed bean paste (*sam jang*) (p 17),
or simply dip barbecued meat in
"BBQ dipping sauce" (p 17).

燒烤醃料一
BARBEQUE MARINADE I

<table>
<tr><td>醬油</td><td>2 大匙</td></tr>
<tr><td>牛肉湯(無亦可)</td><td>2 大匙</td></tr>
<tr><td>麻油</td><td>2 大匙</td></tr>
<tr><td>糖</td><td>1 大匙</td></tr>
<tr><td>蒜末</td><td>2 小匙</td></tr>
<tr><td>胡椒</td><td>1 小匙</td></tr>
</table>

烤牛肉片

1 肋眼牛肉 12 兩(450 公克)切成薄片(圖 1)。可買已切好的牛肉片使用。

2 把攪勻的 ① 料與牛肉抓拌均勻。

3 先將烤爐預熱,將肉烤至兩面微焦即可。

烤牛排骨肉

1 牛排骨去肥油順骨橫切取肉(圖 2)12 兩(450 公克),切成 5 公分寬條,劃刀後再以一刀不斷、一刀斷的方式切成塊狀,拌入攪勻的 ① 料,也可加切碎的奇異果泥 1 小匙及洋蔥泥 2 小匙以增加嫩度,抓拌均勻後即可燒烤食用。

■ 牛排骨肉的油脂比肋眼牛肉多,故較為鮮嫩多汁。

烤牛肉串

牛排骨肉或牛排肉 6 兩(225 公克)切塊,先加入攪勻的 ① 料抓拌均勻,再加切塊的蔬菜 6 兩(225 公克)翻拌,(蔬菜可用香菇、洋蔥、紅蘿蔔及蘆筍等,紅蘿蔔及蘆筍需先川燙過)。肉與蔬菜以竹籤交替串起(圖 3),燒烤後可當前菜。

烤雞肉

去皮雞胸肉 12 兩(450 公克)切塊,加攪勻的 ① 料抓拌均勻醃 1 小時(如可醃一夜味道會更佳),燒烤後即可食用。

- 2 T. soy sauce
- 2 T. beef stock (optional)
- 2 T. sesame oil
- 1 T. sugar
- 2 t. minced garlic cloves
- 1 t. pepper

BEEF BARBEQUE (BULGOGI)

1 Cut 1 lb. (450g) rib eye steak into thin slices (Fig.1). Prepackaged thin slices of beef may be purchased at Korean and most Asian markets.

2 Mix ① thoroughly and marinate the beef.

3 Pre-heat the barbeque grill, then barbeque the meat until both sides turn slightly brown; serve.

SHORT RIBS BARBEQUE (KALBI GUI)

1 Remove fat and cut along the bone of the short ribs (Fig.2) to get 1 lb. (450g) meat. Cut meat into 2" (5 cm) wide strips. Then make an initial crosswise cut half way through each strip, followed by a second cut all the way through until all are cut into pieces. Mix ① thoroughly and marinate the meat. Add 1 t. minced kiwi and 2 t. minced onion to tenderize. Barbeque and serve.

■ Short ribs contain more fat than the rib eye used in "Bulgogi," but some may prefer the tenderness and juicier flavor.

SKEWERED BEEF AND VEGETABLES (SAN JUK)

Cut 1/2 lb. (225g) short ribs or sirloin into bite size pieces. Add ①, mix thoroughly, then mix with 1/2 lb (225g) of cut vegetables, (shiitake mushrooms, onions, blanched carrots and asparagus). Assemble beef and vegetables on skewers by alternating beef and vegetables, (Fig. 3). Barbeque and serve.

Use 1 lb. (450g) skinless chicken breast. Cut to bite size. Add ①, mix thoroughly and marinate with chicken. Marinate for 1 hour; overnight will give stronger flavor. Barbeque and serve.

燒烤醃料二
BARBEQUE MARINADE II

2 - 4 人份 · SERVES 2 - 4

烤豬肉片

1　豬腰肉 12 兩（450 公克）切薄片（圖 1），可買已切好的豬肉片使用。

2　把攪勻的 ① 料與豬肉抓拌均勻略醃。

3　先將烤爐預熱，將肉烤至兩面微焦即可。

■　除了用豬肉薄片外，像豬大排這種大塊肉片可特別選來做為於戶外烤肉時的材料（一般室內烤肉多用切薄片或切小塊）。醃豬大排時整塊用刀背敲鬆或加少許小蘇打粉可增加肉的嫩度，再加 ① 料醃泡一小時或隔夜。

烤羊肉

1　羊腰肉去肥 12 兩（450 公克），先在表面上劃刀，再以一刀斷、一刀不斷的方式切塊以便入味（圖 2），並加攪勻的 ① 料抓拌均勻（圖 3）。

2　先將烤爐預熱，將肉烤至兩面微焦即可。

① 料：
- 醬油 .... 1 大匙
- 韓國辣椒醬 .... 2 大匙
- 麻油 .... 2 大匙
- 糖 .... 2 大匙
- 蒜末 .... 1 大匙
- 胡椒 .... 少許
- 薑末 .... 少許

① ─
- 1 T. soy sauce
- 2 T. hot pepper paste
- 2 T. sesame oil
- 2 T. sugar
- 1 T. minced garlic cloves
- pinch of pepper
- pinch of minced ginger

SPICY PORK BARBEQUE (*DAEJI BULGOGI*)

1　Cut 1 lb. (450g) pork tenderloin into thin slices (Fig.1). Prepackaged thin slices of pork may be purchased in all Korean markets and most Asian markets.

2　Mix ① thoroughly and marinate the pork.

3　Pre-heat the barbeque grill, then barbeque the meat until both sides turn slightly brown; serve.

■　Instead of thin slices, large steaks of lean and boneless pork may be used. This cut is perhaps best suited for an outdoor barbeque rather than on a table top burner. Tenderize the pork by pounding with the back of the knife. A dash of baking soda will also help tenderize the pork. Mix ① thoroughly and marinate for 1 hour or overnight.

SPICY LAMB BARBEQUE (*YANG GUI*)

1　Trim the fat off lamb tenderloin. Use 1 lb. (450g) lamb, then make an initial crosswise cut half way through each strip, followed by a second cut all the way through until all are cut into pieces (Fig. 2). Mix ① thoroughly and marinate the lamb (Fig. 3).

2　Pre-heat the barbeque grill, then barbeque the meat until both sides turn slightly brown; serve.

燒烤醃料三
BARBEQUE MARINADE III

淡色醬油	4 小匙
味醂	½ 小匙
麻油	½ 小匙
糖	2 小匙
蒜末	½ 小匙
白胡椒	⅛ 小匙
橘子汁	½ 小匙
檸檬汁	½ 小匙

1

烤蝦

1 蝦去殼留尾 12 兩 (450 公克),沿蝦背劃一刀 (圖 1) 去蝦泥,再輕輕劃斜刀成交叉紋把攪勻的 ① 料與蝦抓拌均勻。

2 先將烤爐預熱,將蝦烤至兩面微焦即可食用。

烤干貝

1 大干貝 12 兩 (450 公克) 橫切二半 (圖 2)。

2 把攪勻的 ① 料與干貝抓拌均勻,燒烤後即可食用。

烤魷魚

1 魷魚 12 兩 (450 公克) 在內面輕輕劃斜刀成交叉紋,再切片 (圖 3)。

2 把攪勻的 ① 料與魷魚抓拌均勻,燒烤後即可食。

4 t. soy sauce
½ t. mirin
½ t. sesame oil
2 t. sugar
½ t. minced garlic clove
⅛ t. white pepper
½ t. orange juice
½ t. lemon juice

1

SHRIMP BARBEQUE (*SE WOO GUI*)

1 Use 1 lb. (450g) shelled shrimp, (keep the tail intact). Cut along the back of the shrimp (Fig.1), just deep enough to expose and discard the dark intestinal tract . Mix ① thoroughly and marinate the shrimp.

2 Pre-heat the barbeque grill, then barbeque the shrimp until both sides turn slightly brown; serve .

SCALLOP BARBEQUE (*GARIBI GUI*)

1 Use 1 lb. (450g) large scallops, laterally slice each into 2 pieces (Fig.2).

2 Mix ① thoroughly and marinate the scallops. Barbeque and serve.

SQUID BARBEQUE (*O JING AW GUI*)

1 Use 1 lb. (450g) squid, score diagonal cuts to form a criss-cross diamond pattern. Cut them into wide strips, then slice. (Fig.3).

2 Mix ① thoroughly and marinate the squid. Barbeque and serve.

紅燒鱈魚
SPICY BLACK COD (EUN DAE GU JO RIM)

帶皮鱈魚肉 *...12 兩(450 公克)
白蘿蔔(與魚片同大小).......1 片

1.
魚高湯(見 8 頁)....................3 杯
醬油.................................¼ 杯
糖...................................2 大匙
味醂、韓國辣椒粉......各 1 大匙

2.
辣椒、蔥、蒜......略切共 3 大匙

1 lb. (450g) black cod fillet
  with skin*
1 piece of daikon (same size
  as black cod fillet)

1.
3 c. anchovy stock (p.8)
¼ c. soy sauce
2 T. sugar
1 T. ea.: mirin, red pepper
  powder

2.
3 T. total (cut in pieces):
  jalapeno, green onion,
  garlic cloves

1 白蘿蔔上置魚片,放入鍋內(圖 1),隨入 ① 及 ② 料,鍋底不要太大,以便湯汁能略蓋滿魚,煮魚時不需翻動。

2 煮開後蓋鍋續煮 15 分鐘,再改中火續煮約 30 分鐘,煮至汁略收乾(如見湯汁很多,中途去鍋蓋改用大火,小心勿煮太乾以免燒焦)。此道菜味道香濃。

★ 可用石班或其他鮮魚。

1 Put fish on top of daikon and place in a small pot (Fig.1) then add ① and ②, sauce should be enough to cover the fish, no need to turn fish over during cooking.

2 Bring to boil; cover and cook 15 minutes. Reduce heat to medium; continue to cook for approximately 30 minutes until liquid is almost evaporated (If remaining liquid is excessive, increase heat and cook uncovered until juices are almost gone, but not too dry or burnt). This is a very flavorful and tasty dish.

★ Grouper may also be used.

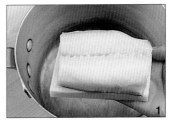

烤魚片
BROILED SEASONED FISH (YANG NUM SANG SUN)

新鮮魚片.........12 兩(450 公克)
鹽............................. ½ 小匙

1.
醬油、糖....................各 2 大匙
韓國辣椒醬、麻油......各 1 大匙
洋蔥末...1 大匙,蒜末....2 小匙
炒芝麻...1 小匙,白胡椒... 少許

1 lb. (450g) white fish fillet
½ t. salt

1.
2 T. ea.: soy sauce, sugar
1 T. ea.: hot pepper paste (go
  chu jang), sesame oil
1 T. minced onion
2 t. minced garlic cloves
1 t. toasted sesame seeds,
  pinch of white pepper

1 在魚片上交叉劃斜刀,撒上鹽,醃 30 分鐘。

2 烤箱燒熱,將魚置於烤盤內,把拌勻的 ① 料淋在魚上,以 300˚F(150˚C)烤 20 分鐘後,改 500˚F(260˚C)烤至金黃色肉熟即可。餘汁可淋在魚上。

■ 魚的種類可選龍利、石班或鮭魚等;拌料 ① 的味道很好,可用來炒蝦、魷魚或其他肉類。

1 Make diagonal crisscross cuts on the fish fillet. Sprinkle on salt and let sit 30 minutes.

2 Pre-heat oven. Place fish on baking pan; pour mixture ① on fish. Bake 20 minutes at 300˚F (150˚C); increase heat to 500˚F (260˚C). Bake until cooked and golden brown. Pour remaining juice on top of fish.

■ For fish selection; choose sole, grouper or salmon. Mixture ① makes a great sauce and may be used to stir-fry shrimp, squid or other meat.

紅燒雞腿
BRAISED SPICY CHICKEN (*DAK DO RI TANG*)

雞腿(切塊).......12 兩(450 公克)

① ┌ 蒜.............................6 粒
　　馬鈴薯 * 、紅蘿蔔..................
　　└ ....切塊共 6 兩(225 公克)

② ┌ 罐頭雞湯、水.............各 1 杯
　　醬油.............................4 小匙
　　└ 糖、韓國辣椒粉.........各 2 小匙

③ ┌ 洋蔥.......1 片,蔥.............6 段

1 雞塊在滾水內川燙撈出拭乾水份。

2 油 2 小匙燒熱,將雞塊略煎再炒至金黃色加入 ① 料略炒,再加 ② 料煮開,改小火加蓋煮 15 分鐘(若湯汁剩太多,大火燒煮至汁略收乾), 再放入 ③ 料煮 5 分鐘即可。

* 若用新出的小馬鈴薯更佳,不需切塊。

---

1 lb. (450g) chicken thighs, cut in pieces

① ┌ **6 garlic cloves**
　　½ lb. (225g) total (cut in
　　└ **pieces): potatoes*, carrots**

② ┌ **1 c. ea.: canned chicken broth, water**
　　4 t. soy sauce
　　2 t. ea.: sugar, red pepper powder

③ ┌ **1 slice onion**
　　└ **6 green onion sections**

1 Blanch chicken in boiling water; drain and pat dry.

2 Heat 2 t.oil; pan-fry chicken then stir-fry until golden brown. Add ① and lightly stir, add ② and bring to boil. Reduce heat to low, cover and cook 15 minutes. (If too much liquid remains, remove cover and use high heat until liquid is almost evaporated). Add ③, cook 5 minutes; serve.

* For best results, use baby potatoes; no need to cut in pieces.

紅燒牛排骨
SHORT RIBS STEW (*KAL BI CHIM*)

牛排骨.............1½ 斤(900 公克)

① ┌ 紅、白蘿蔔(1 公分厚)....各 2 片
　　└ 新鮮香菇...2 朵,銀杏.......6 粒

② ┌ 水.............................4 杯
　　味醂、玉米糖漿...........各 1 大匙
　　醬油、糖.......................各 ½ 杯
　　肉桂條、麻油、蒜末..各 ½ 大匙
　　└ 薑片、蔥段...............各 2 大匙

1 將牛排骨(圖 1)肉面上劃刀,並順著牛骨切條 後再切塊,在多量滾水內川燙撈出。

2 鍋內放入牛排骨及 ② 料,煮開後續煮 20 分 鐘,再入 ① 料煮開改小火再煮 10 分鐘,用太 白粉 ½ 小匙,加水 1 大匙芶芡,即可上桌。

---

2 lbs. (900g) short ribs

① ┌ **2 slices (½", 1 cm thick) ea.: carrot, daikon**
　　2 shiitake mushrooms
　　└ **6 gingkoes**

② ┌ **4 c. water**
　　1 T. ea.: mirin, corn syrup
　　½ c. ea.: soy sauce, sugar
　　½ T. ea.: cinnamon stick, sesame oil, minced garlic clove
　　└ **2 T. ea.: ginger slices, sectioned green onions**

1 Score short ribs (Fig.1) with crisscross cuts on each piece; cut into strips then pieces; blanch in plenty of boiling water.

2 Put short ribs and ② in sauce pan; bring to boil for 20 minutes. Add ①, reduce to low heat and cook for 10 minutes. Mix 1 T. water and ½ t. starch, then add to stew to thicken. Serve.

1

韓式五更腸旺
SPICY BEEF ORGAN STEW (GOP CHANG JUNGOAL)

牛腸	淨重 12 兩(450 公克)
百葉	3 兩(115 公克)
① 薑	1 片，料酒 * ½ 杯
水	10 杯
麻油	3 大匙
② 洋蔥(切碎)	½ 個
韓國辣椒醬	1 大匙，豆瓣醬 ½ 大匙
蒜末	1 小匙，薑末 ½ 小匙
③ 韓國西洋菜(切段)	2 杯
蔥(切段)	4 枝，洋蔥(切片) ½ 個
紅蘿蔔(切片)	½ 條
金針菇及粉絲	各 1 小把
大白菜(切塊)	2 片，豆腐 4 塊
④ 牛高湯(見 8 頁)	3 杯
醬油	1 大匙
味醂、糖	各 1 小匙
韓國辣椒粉	2 大匙

1 將牛腸及百葉加入 ① 料煮開，續煮 1 小時煮至牛腸及百葉均軟熟，撈出冷卻後切 5 公分長段，湯汁倒出不要。

2 麻油燒熱，放入 ② 料炒香，加入煮熟的牛腸及百葉，再入 ③ 料及 ④ 料。

3 煮開後續煮 5 分鐘，食時連鍋端出。

* 料酒(SOJU) 是一種特製的蒸餾酒，由 94 % 的大麥芽酒、4% 的麥酒及 2% 的米酒所提煉。(酒精濃度為 24%)(圖 1)。

■ 一般食用時，會將小型爐與鍋端上桌。吃剩的湯汁，可再加入麵條煮食。

---

1 lb. (450g) beef intestines
¼ lb. (115g) tripe
① 1 ginger slice
½ c. soju* (Korean liquor)
10 c. water

3 T. sesame oil
② ½ onion, minced
1 T. hot pepper paste (go chu jang)
½ T. soybean paste (den jang)
1 t. minced garlic clove
½ t. minced ginger

③ 2 c. Korean watercress, sectioned
4 green onions, sectioned
½ ea.(sliced): onion, carrot
enoki mushrooms and glass
**   noodles as desired**
2 napa cabbage leaves, cut in
**   pieces**
4 pieces tofu

④ 3 c. beef broth (p.8)
1 T. soy sauce
1 t. ea.: mirin, sugar
2 T. red pepper powder

1 Boil intestines and tripe in ① for 1 hour until intestines and tripe soften. Remove intestines and tripe; let cool and cut into 2" (5cm) sections, discard liquid.

2 Heat sesame oil and stir-fry ②, then add intestines, tripe, ③ and ④.

3 Bring to a boil and cook for 5 minutes; serve.

* soju (Korean liquor) is a distilled spirit, made with 94% grain neutral spirits, 4% grain spirits and 2% rice spirits. (24% alcohol concentration) (Fig.1).

■ This dish may be served in a hot pot with a table-top burner to keep the dish hot while being served. Toward the end of the dish, much of the goodies may be eaten with the broth remaining. Noodles may be added to the broth and eaten while being cooked.

辣味海鮮煲
SPICY SEAFOOD STEW *(ME OON TANG)*

① ┌ 魚高湯 *(見 8 頁)..............3 杯
　├ 韓國辣椒醬................1⅓ 大匙
　└ 韓國辣椒粉、蒜末..各 ½ 小匙
② ┌ 大白菜(切塊)....................2 片
　├ 白蘿蔔..............................6 片
　├ 蛤蜊........6 個，蝦........2 隻
　├ 豆腐(4 片)，鮮魚肉(切片).......
　└ ....共 12 兩(450 公克)
③ ┌ 金針菇、唐好菜、蔥段各 ¼ 杯

① ┌ 3 c. anchovy stock* (p.8)
　├ 1⅓ T. hot pepper paste (go
　│　chu jang)
　├ ½ t. ea.: red pepper powder,
　└　minced garlic clove
② ┌ 2 leaves of napa cabbage,
　│　cut in pieces
　├ 6 daikon slices
　├ 6 manila clams, 2 shrimp
　├ 1lb. (450g) total(sliced): 4
　└　tofu, fish fillets
③ ┌ ¼ c. ea.: enoki mushrooms,
　│　green leafy vegetable,
　└　sectioned green onion

1 將 ①、②(圖 1)及 ③ 料，置鍋內煮開後續煮
　10 分鐘，即可食用。

* 若無魚高湯，可在清水內加數條魚乾代替。

■ 此種湯海鮮煮開後再煮 10 分鐘，湯才夠味，
　適合在冬天連鍋上桌邊煮邊食。② 料內的鮮
　魚肉可用石斑、鱸魚或其他新鮮魚，也可用魚
　頭或整條魚。

1 Boil ①, ② (Fig.1) and ③; continue to cook 10
　minutes; serve.

* If anchovy stock is not available, add several
　dried anchovies to the water as an alternative.

■ It is important to cook 10 more minutes after
　boiling to enhance the flavor of the soup. This
　dish is particularly good in winter as a hot pot
　dish to be eaten while cooking.Red snapper,
　black sea bass, fish head or whole fish may be
　used for fish fillets of ②.

蛤蜊豆腐煲
SPICY TOFU STEW WITH CLAMS *(SOON DU BOO)*

① ┌ 嫩豆腐.....1 斤 2 兩(675 公克)
　├ 蛤蜊(小).........................10 個
　└ 中蝦..................................2 隻
② ┌ 蛤蜊精(見 14 頁)..........1 小匙
　├ 韓國辣椒粉、鹽、油各 1 小匙
　└ 魚高湯 *(見 8 頁)..............1 杯
③ ┌ 蔥花、紫菜絲..........各 1 大匙

① ┌ 1½ lbs. (675g) soft tofu
　├ 10 small manila clams
　└ 2 medium shrimp
② ┌ 1 t. clam bouillon (p.14)
　├ 1 t. ea: red pepper powder,
　│　salt, oil
　└ 1 c. anchovy stock*(p.8)
③ ┌ 1 T. ea.: chopped green
　│　onions, shredded
　└　seaweed (kim)

1 將 ① 料(圖 2)及 ② 料燒開續用大火不加蓋煮
　10 分鐘後，撒上 ③ 料後連鍋端出。

* 若無魚高湯，可在清水內加數條魚乾代替。

1 Bring ① (Fig.2) and ② to boil, continue to cook
　over high heat (uncovered) for 10 minutes.
　Sprinkle ③ on top and serve.

*If anchovy stock is not available, add several
　dried anchovies to the water as an alternative.

泡菜豆腐煲
KIMCHI STEW (*KIMCHI CHI GE*)

2 人份 · SERVES 2

1 ┌ 韓國泡菜(不洗).............1½ 杯
  └ 蒜末.........................¼ 小匙
    豬肉(切片).....................½ 杯
2 ┌ 牛肉精(見 14 頁)、韓國辣椒
  └ 粉...........................各 ¼ 小匙
3 ┌ 豆腐(切塊).......4 兩(150 公克)
  └ 魚高湯 *(見 8 頁).............2 杯

1 油 1 大匙燒熱,將 1 料略炒,放入豬肉片、2 及 3 料燒開再煮 10 分鐘連鍋端出。

* 若無魚高湯,可在清水內加數條魚乾代替。

1 ┌ 1½ c. kimchi (do not rinse)
  └ ¼ t. minced garlic clove
    ½ c. lean pork, sliced
2 ┌ ¼ t. beef bouillon (p.14)
  └ ¼ t. red pepper powder
3 ┌ ⅓ lb. (150g) tofu, cut in
  │   pieces
  └ 2 c. anchovy stock* (p.8)

1 Heat 1 T. oil, stir-fry 1 briefly in a pot. Add pork, 2 and 3, bring to boil and cook for 10 minutes. Serve in the pot.

*If anchovy stock is not available, add several dried anchovies to the water as an alternative.

牛肉豆腐煲
BEEF AND BEAN PASTE STEW (*DEN JANG CHI GE*)

2 人份 · SERVES 2

    牛肉(切丁).....................½ 杯
  ┌ 魚高湯 *(見 8 頁).............1 杯
1 │ 豆瓣醬.........................2 大匙
  └ 韓國辣椒醬...................1 小匙
2 □ 2 料同上
  ┌ 豆腐(切丁).....................1 杯
3 │ 意大利瓜、蔥、洋蔥、毛菇、
  └ 韓國辣椒.............切丁各 ⅓ 杯

1 將牛肉、1 及 2 料放入鍋內煮開,煮滾 5 分鐘,再入 3 料,燒開後加蓋煮 5 分鐘即可。

* 若無魚高湯,可在清水內加數條魚乾代替。

■ 豆腐煲不必煎炒,煮好後連鍋上桌,簡單又好吃。適合忙碌的上班族。

    ½ c. beef, diced
  ┌ 1 c. anchovy stock* (p.8)
  │ 2 T. soybean paste (den
1 │   jang)
  │ 1 t. hot pepper paste (go
  └   chu jang)
2 □ Same as above recipe
  ┌ 1 c. (diced) tofu
  │ ⅓ c. ea.(diced): zucchini,
3 │   green onions, onions,
  │   mushrooms, Korean chili
  └   peppers

1 Bring 1, 2 and beef to boil in a pot; cook 5 minutes. Add 3, bring to boil. Cover and cook 5 more minutes. Serve in the pot.

* If anchovy stock is not available, add several dried anchovies to the water as an alternative.

■ This dish is delicious and very easy to make. After cooking, simply serve directly in the pot at the table.

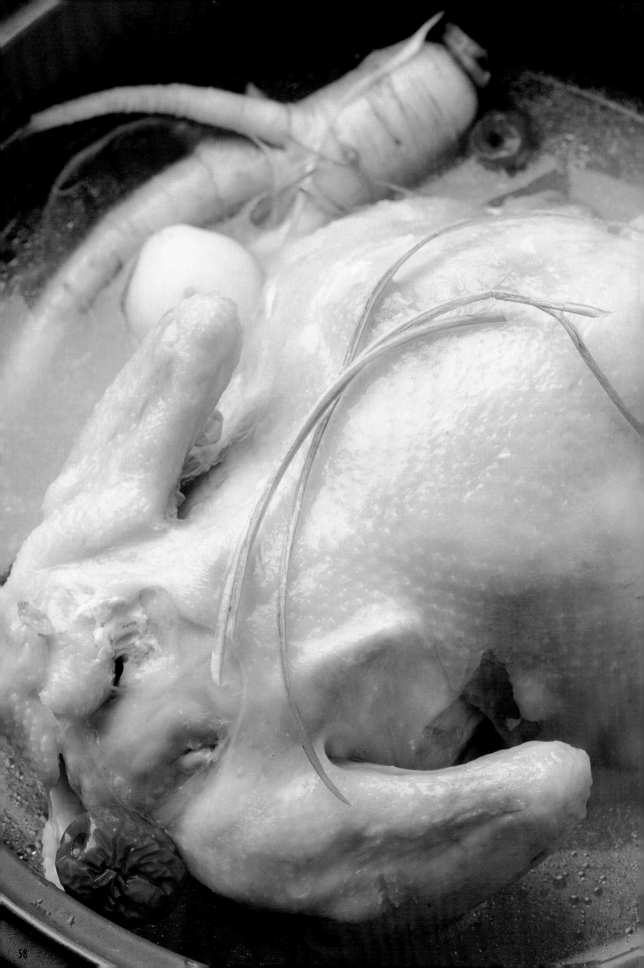

人蔘雞湯
GINSENG CHICKEN SOUP *(SAM GAE TANG)*

	小種雞 2 隻..1½ 斤(900 公克)	
⓵	糯米(泡 1 小時)............4 大匙	
	新鮮粟子(乾的也可) ....4 個	
	紅棗(大) ....4 個	
	蒜...6 瓣	
	高麗蔘 ....1 條	
⓶	鹽 ....¾ 小匙	
	胡椒 ....⅛ 小匙	
	蔥花 ....2 大匙	
⓷	鹽 ....1 大匙	
	胡椒、炒芝麻..........各 ¼ 小匙	

1 將 ⓵ 料拌勻分成 2 份，分別填入 2 隻小雞內 (圖 1)，為避免餡料漏出來，在一隻腿上切開一個洞，把另一隻腿穿過去成交叉狀(圖 2)。

2 水 10 杯燒開，放入填好的 2 隻雞(水需滿過雞身)煮開後，改中火蓋鍋煮約 1½ 小時，湯汁若剩太多，中途去蓋用大火煮至湯汁剩 3 杯，加入 ⓶ 料，分盛於 2 個大碗，並撒上蔥花。食時雞肉可沾拌勻的 ⓷ 料。

■ 人參雞湯是韓國的傳統菜餚，平時配一些小菜，即可當餐，不僅好吃，亦可用來冬補。

⓵
- 2 Cornish game hens, 2 lbs. (900g)
- 4 T. sweet rice (soaked for 1 hour)
- 4 chestnuts (or dried)
- 4 large dried red dates
- 6 garlic cloves
- 1 ginseng

⓶
- ¾ t. salt
- ⅛ t. pepper
- 2 T. chopped green onions

⓷
- 1 T. salt
- ¼ t. ea.: pepper, toasted sesame seeds

1 Mix ⓵, stuff each Cornish hen with ½ of mixture ⓵ (Fig.1). Cut a slot through the skin of one leg and pass the other leg through the slot to hold in the filling for each hen (Fig.2).

2 Boil 10 cups of water. Immerse hens in the boiling water. Be sure water covers the hens completely. When water boils again, reduce heat to medium; cover and cook 1½ hours. If too much liquid remains, uncover and raise heat to high; check liquid while cooking until only three cups of liquid remain. Add ⓶ and divide to two bowls; sprinkle with the onions. Serve. Use mixed ⓷ to dip hens in.

■ This is considered a one-dish meal. It is not only tasty, but also highly nutritional. Stuffed ginseng chicken is usually served during summers and winters, and is believed to have a rejuvenating effect.

牛肉冬粉湯

SPICY BEEF AND VEGETABLE SOUP *(YOOK KAE JANG)*

牛瘦肉...............9 兩(340 公克)

①
- 油、麻油...................各 2 大匙
- 韓國辣椒粉.....................2 大匙
- 西式紅椒粉、黑胡椒 .各 ½ 小匙
- 鹽.............................2½ 小匙
- 蒜末..............................2 小匙

②
- 綠豆芽、蔥段...............各 2 杯
- 蠔菇(略撕).........................2 杯

蛋(打散)..............................2 個

乾冬粉..............1.5 兩(56 公克)

1　10 杯水燒開放入牛肉再煮開，改小火蓋鍋煮 1½ 小時，取出用手撕成絲(圖 1)，取肉湯 8 杯備用。

2　水燒開熄火，將冬粉放入，泡 5 分鐘後撈出，再用清水漂涼瀝乾可得 1 杯。

3　撕過的牛肉絲拌入 ① 及 ② 料，略用手攪拌使入味，再與肉湯 8 杯煮開，煮 10 分鐘後續加冬粉及打散的蛋，立即可食。

■ 若喜歡牛肉湯味濃，則煮牛肉時加一些罐頭牛高湯。

¾ lb. (340g) lean beef

①
- 2 T. ea.: oil, sesame oil, red pepper powder
- ½ t. paprika
- ½ t. black pepper
- 2 ½ t. salt
- 2 t. minced garlic cloves

②
- 2 c. ea.: mung bean sprouts, sectioned green onions
- 2 c. oyster mushrooms (slightly shredded)

2 eggs, beaten

2 oz. (56g) glass noodles

1　Boil 10 c. water; immerse beef and bring to boil again. Reduce heat to low, cover and cook 11/2 hours. Remove beef and shred by hand (Fig.1). Set aside beef and 8 c. broth.

2　Boil water, then turn off heat, add glass noodles and soak for 5 minutes until soft. Drain and set aside.

3　Mix shredded beef with ① and ②. Use hands to mix and rub until seasonings are fully absorbed. Add 8 c. broth and boil for 10 minutes. Add glass noodles and slowly add beaten eggs. Immediately turn off heat and serve.

■ If stronger beef flavor is preferred, add canned beef broth.

海 帶 芽 湯

SEAWEED SOUP *(MIYUK KUK)*

海帶芽.........................2 大匙

牛高湯(見 8 頁)..................3 杯

麻油..............................½ 小匙

1　海帶芽洗淨泡水瀝乾 (圖 2)，略切 ½ 杯備用。

2　麻油燒熱，放入海帶芽略炒加高湯燒滾即成。

2 T. dried seaweed (miyuk)

3 c. beef broth (p.8)

½ t. sesame oil

1　Wash seaweed, then soak in cold water until soft (Fig.2); drain. Cut seaweed into coarse pieces to get ½ cup; set aside.

2　Heat sesame oil and lightly stir-fry seaweed; add beef broth and bring to boil. Serve.

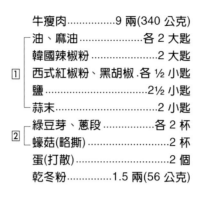

豆瓣菠菜湯
SPINACH AND CLAM SOUP *(SI KUM CHI DEN JANG KUK)*

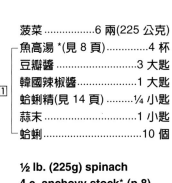

菠菜 ....6 兩(225 公克)
┌ 魚高湯 *(見 8 頁)............4 杯
│ 豆瓣醬 ....3 大匙
│ 韓國辣椒醬...................1 大匙
① 蛤蜊精(見 14 頁) ....¼ 小匙
│ 蒜末 ....1 小匙
└ 蛤蜊................................10 個

½ lb. (225g) spinach
┌ 4 c. anchovy stock* (p.8)
│ 3 T. soybean paste (den jang)
│ 1 T. hot pepper paste (go chu jang)
① ¼ t. clam bouillon (p.14)
│ 1 t. minced garlic clove
└ 10 little neck or Manila clams

1 水略蓋滿蛤蜊置 30 分鐘(圖 1)，吐沙後撈出；菠菜略切備用。

2 將 ① 料放入鍋中，燒開煮至蛤蜊開口，隨即放入菠菜再煮滾即可。

* 若無魚高湯，可在清水內加數條魚乾代替。

1 Place clams in cold water for 30 minutes to release sand (Fig.1), then drain. Cut spinach in large sections.

2 Bring 1 to boil, continue to cook until clams open. Add spinach, bring to boil again; serve.

*If anchovy stock is not available, add several dried anchovies to the water as an alternative.

蛤蜊清湯
CLEAR CLAM SOUP *(JO KAE TANG)*

蛤蜊...............18 兩(675 公克)
┌ 黑胡椒..............................少許
① 蒜末 ....¼ 小匙
└ 蛤蜊精(見 14 頁) ....¼ 小匙
蔥花 ....1 大匙

1½ lb. (675g) little neck clams
┌ pinch of black pepper
① ¼ t. minced garlic clove
└ ¼ t. clam bouillon (p.14)
1 T. chopped green onion

1 水略蓋滿蛤蜊置 30 分鐘，吐沙後撈出備用。

2 將蛤蜊放入鍋內加 5 杯水燒開，去除泡沫再煮 5 分鐘讓鮮味進入湯內再加 ① 料，灑上蔥花即可。

1 Place clams in cold water for 30 minutes to release sand, then drain.

2 Boil clams with 5 c. water. Skim off foam and continue to boil at high heat until clams open (approximately 5 mins.) Add ①, sprinkle chopped green onion on top. Serve.

什錦菜飯
RICE MEDLEY (BIBIM BAP)

牛肉絲(或絞肉)...............⅓ 杯
1 ┌ 醬油、麻油、糖......各 ½ 小匙
  └ 胡椒、蒜末 ....各少許
麻油 ....1 小匙
2 ┌ 新鮮香菇(切絲) ....4 朵
  └ 紅蘿蔔、黃瓜(切絲) ...各 ½ 杯
3 ┌ 涼拌菠菜(見 83 頁) ....1 杯
  │ 涼拌蘿蔔絲、涼拌豆芽菜
  └ (見 81 、 83 頁) ....各 ½ 杯
蛋(煎荷包蛋).....................2 個
生菜絲 ....1 杯
菜飯辣醬 (見 17 頁)......2 大匙
飯 ....2 碗

1 牛肉拌入 1 料，鍋燒熱(因 1 料有油，不需另外加油)，將肉炒至變色盛出。

2 麻油 1 小匙加熱，依序放入 2 料，加入少許的鹽大火略炒盛出。

3 每一碗飯上，分別置牛肉、 2 及 3 料(圖 1)、煎蛋、生菜、菜飯辣醬，並淋少許麻油。

■ 菜飯在韓國人的家庭非常普遍，利用現有的小菜及菜飯辣醬，即可當餐。在小攤上也有賣，方便給吃了就走的客人。

⅓ c. shredded beef (or ground beef)
1 ┌ ½ t. ea.: soy sauce, sesame oil, sugar
  └ pepper, minced garlic clove as desired
1 t. sesame oil
2 ┌ 4 shiitake mushrooms, shredded
  └ ½ c. ea.(shredded): carrots, cucumber
3 ┌ 1 c. spinach salad (P.83)
  │ ½ c. ea.: spicy daikon salad, bean sprout salad (pp.81,83)
2 fried eggs (over easy)
1 c. shredded lettuce
2 T. hot sauce (p.17)
2 bowls cooked rice

1 Mix 1 with beef. Heat frying pan (oil is not needed as it is in 1 already), and stir mixture until color changes.

2 Heat 1 t. sesame oil. Add 2 in order listed with a pinch of salt. Stir-fry over high heat and set aside.

3 Take 2 bowls of rice, add to each, fried meat, 2, 3 (Fig.1), eggs, lettuce and hot sauce. Sprinkle on sesame oil and serve.

■ Rice Medley is extremely popular to the typical Korean family. Use left over side dishes and hot sauce that can serve as simple family dishes. There are some booths and open markets where you can purchase the rice medley and eat on the spot.

五穀飯
FIVE GRAIN RICE *(O KOK BAP)*

1 ┌ 糯米 ....1 杯
└ 任選三種穀類 * ....各 ⅓ 杯
   紅豆 ....⅓ 杯

1 ┌ 1 c. sweet rice
  │ ⅓ c.ea.: three kinds of
  └   grains*
     ⅓ c. red beans

1 將 1 料(圖 1)洗淨，撈出，重新加水泡 1 小時撈出。

2 紅豆(圖 1)加水不加蓋煮開，轉小火，煮至紅豆熟軟，撈出紅豆備用。(餘汁不用，以免顏色太深)

3 泡好的 1 料及已煮過的紅豆加 2 杯水放入電鍋內煮熟即可。

* 穀類可選擇薏米、小米、高粱、蕎麥或其它。

1 Wash and rinse 1 (Fig.1), then soak in cold water for 1 hour; drain.

2 Boil red beans (Fig.1)in water uncovered; reduce heat to low and cook until done, discard remaining liquid, since it will darken the color of the dish.

3 Combine soaked grains and cooked red beans with 2 c. water, stir and bring to boil; reduce heat to low and continue to cook until the rice is done. For convenience, electric rice cooker may be used.

* Non-glutinous millet, glutinous millets, Indian millets, or other kinds of grains may be used.

黃豆芽飯
RICE WITH SOYBEAN SPROUTS *(KONG NA MUL BAP)*

   米 ....1½ 杯
   黃豆芽(去根)...6 兩(225 公克)
1 ┌ 水 ....2 杯
└ 鹽 ....少許

   1½ c. rice
   ½ lb. (225g) soybean
      sprouts (roots removed)
1 ┌ 2 c. water
  └ pinch of salt

1 米洗淨泡水 1 小時撈出，拌入黃豆芽及 1 料放入電鍋內煮成飯即成。

■ 黃豆芽飯適合與烤牛肉（見 45 頁）並淋少許"煎餅沾醬"（見 16 頁)食用。

1 Wash rice thoroughly with cold water, soak for 1 hour; drain. Mix rice with soybean sprouts and 1, cover and bring to boil. Simmer until cooked. For convenience, electric rice cooker may be used.

■ Serve with "Beef Barbeque" (Bul Go Gui) (p.45) and pancake sauce (p.16).

韓式壽司
KOREAN STYLE SUSHI (*KIM BAP*)

米..........................1 杯
① ┌ 麻油、芝麻................. 各 1 小匙
　 └ 鹽.............................½ 小匙
② ┌ 牛肉絲.........................¾ 杯
　 │ 燙熟菠菜(葉帶莖)............16 片
　 │ 燙熟紅蘿蔔、小黃瓜、醃黃蘿
　 │ 蔔...........(1×1×20 公分)各 2 條
　 └ 蛋(煎成蛋皮切粗條).........2 個
③ ┌ 鹽...½ 小匙，麻油....... 1½ 小匙
紫菜............................2 張

1 c. rice
① ┌ 1 t. ea.: sesame oil, sesame
　 │ 　　seeds
　 └ ½ t. salt
　 ┌ ¾ c. shredded beef
　 │ 16 spinach (leaves and
　 │ 　　stems), pre-blanched
② │ 2 sticks (½"×½"×8",
　 │ 　　1×1×20cm)ea.: pre-boiled
　 │ 　　carrots, cucumber, and
　 │ 　　preserved pickled radish
　 └ 2 eggs (scramble then shred)
③ ┌ ½ t. salt, 1½ t. sesame oil
2 nori sheets

1 米按照包裝上的指示煮成飯後，拌入 ① 料分成 2 份，待冷備用。

2 將 ② 料內的牛肉絲拌入一半的 ③ 料炒熟，菠菜拌入另一半的 ③ 料，小黃瓜用 ¼ 小匙鹽略醃。全部 ② 料分成 2 份。

3 竹簾上放一片紫菜，在 ¾ 的位置將一份飯鋪平，續放入一份 ② 料(圖 1)，由竹簾一邊捲起呈圓筒狀。可當主菜或前菜。

1 Cook rice by following cooking instructions on the rice bag. Mix ①. Divide into two portions and let cool; set aside.

2 Prepare ② as follows: Mix half of ③ with shredded beef; stir-fry, set aside. Then mix spinach with the remaining half of ③. Marinade cucumber in ¼ t. salt. Divide ② into 2 portions.

3 Place 1 piece of nori on a bamboo mat and cover ¾ of the nori with rice; flatten rice; then place on one portion of ② (Fig.1). Enclose in nori by rolling it up to form a cylinder. This dish makes an excellent main dish or appetizer.

生魚飯
SASHIMI RICE (*HWE DUP BAP*)

鮪魚(切片).........9 兩(340 公克)
① ┌ 飯......2 碗，麻油............2 小匙
　 │ 生菜絲.............................1 杯
　 └ 小黃瓜片..........................½ 杯
② ┌ 白蘿蔔絲..........................1 杯
　 └ 紫菜絲.............................2 小匙
酸辣沾醬(見 16 頁)............適量

¾ lb. (340g), tuna (diced)
　 ┌ 2 c. cooked rice
　 │ 2 t. sesame oil
① │ 1 c. shredded lettuce
　 └ ½ c. cucumber slices
② ┌ 1 c. shredded daikon
　 └ 2 t. seaweed (kim)
sour & hot sauce (p.16) as
　　desired

1 將 ② 料的白蘿蔔絲浸放於冷水中 5 分鐘，撈出瀝乾。

2 依序將 ① 料、鮪魚片及 ② 料分盛在二個碗內，與"酸辣沾醬"拌食。

1 Soak shredded daikon of ② in cold water for 5 minutes; drain.

2 Divide all the ingredients equally in 2 bowls by first placing ①, then tuna, and finally ②. Serve with sour and hot sauce.

鮑魚粥
ABALONE PORRIDGE

米..............................½ 杯
麻油.............................1 小匙
鮑魚(切片).......................½ 杯
①⎡蛋黃..........1 個，鹽.......½ 小匙
②⎡新鮮香菇、紅蘿蔔、蘆筍.........
　⎣...........................(切碎)各 ½ 大匙
紫菜絲...........................1 大匙

1 將米浸泡在清水內 3 小時至米粒漲大時撈出，與 3 杯水放入果汁機內略打成米漿(不必打太細)。

2 麻油燒熱放入鮑魚(圖 1)炒至變色，加入米漿燒滾再改用中火，煮時需邊攪拌以免粘鍋，煮至濃稠狀。

3 將 ① 料及 ② 料依序放入粥內，攪拌煮 1 分鐘，分盛 2 碗上撒紫菜絲，趁熱與小菜配食。

■ 粥的味道清淡適於胃口欠佳時食用。有新鮮鮑魚最好，若無可用罐頭鮑魚、其他海鮮或雞肉取代。用飯煮粥，水與飯的比例是 3 比 1。

½ c. rice
1 t. sesame oil
½ c. abalone, slices
①⎡1 egg yolk
　⎣½ t. salt
②⎡½ T. ea.(chopped): shiitake
　⎢　mushrooms, carrots,
　⎣　asparagus
1 T. shredded seaweed (kim)

1 Soak rice in cold water 3 hours until it expands. Slightly blend rice with 3 c. water in a blender.

2 Heat sesame oil; stir-fry abalone (Fig.1) until color is changed. Add blended rice and bring to boil. Reduce heat to medium, cook until thickened. Stir continuously to avoid sticking to pan.

3 Add in ① to ② in the order listed to porridge; cook and stir for 1 minute. Divide to 2 bowls; sprinkle on kim and serve hot with side dish.

■ The flavor is very light and is suitable whenever there is any stomach discomfort. The use of fresh abalone gives the best results. May substitute with canned abalone, other seafood or chicken meat. If cooked rice is used, water to rice proportions are 3 to 1.

松子粥
PINE NUT PORRIDGE (JAT JOOK)

米..............................6 大匙
①⎡松子.............................6 大匙
　⎣水..............................3 杯
鹽..............................½ 小匙

1 將米浸泡在清水內 3 小時至米粒漲大即撈出，連同 ① 料放入果汁機內打成很細並過濾成松子米漿。

2 松子米漿倒入鍋內煮開，改中火，需攪拌以免粘鍋，煮至稀糊狀，隨加鹽分盛 2 碗，依喜好撒入數粒松子做為裝飾，可配較清淡的小菜趁熱食用。

6 T. rice
①⎡6 T. pine nuts
　⎣3 c. water
½ t. salt

1 Soak rice in cold water for 3 hours until it expands. Place soaked rice and ① in blender and grind to fine; strain.

2 Place ground mixture in saucepan, bring to boil. Cook over medium heat; stir continuously to avoid sticking and cook until slightly thick. Add salt and divide to 2 bowls. Sprinkle on pine nuts for garnish. Serve with a mild side dish.

豆漿麵線

SOMEN WITH SOYBEAN MILK (KONG KUK SOO)

黃豆............................1 杯
鹽................................隨意
炒芝麻........................2 大匙
麵線..................6 兩(225 公克)
黃瓜(切絲)....................½ 杯

1 黃豆泡在溫水內 4 小時至黃豆漲大、皮脫落時，去皮洗淨撈出，隨加 7 杯水煮滾，再改中火續煮 10 分鐘至豆子熟不爛即加鹽熄火。

2 炒芝麻、煮好的豆子及煮汁，全部放入果汁機內打成豆漿，過濾後冰涼(6 杯)。

3 多量水煮開，將麵線煮熟撈出，放入冷水內沖涼，盤捲成 2 糰分盛在 2 個碗內淋入冰豆漿，上面放黃瓜絲，適於炎夏食用。

1 c. soybeans
salt as desired
2 T. toasted sesame seeds
½ lb.(225g) somen
½ c. shredded cucumber

1 Soak soybeans in warm water 4 hours until soybeans expand, and the skin comes off. Remove skin from water and drain. Add 7 c. water; bring to boil. Reduce heat to medium, and cook 10 minutes until beans are just cooked, then add salt.

2 Place toasted sesame seeds, cooked beans and cooked juice in a blender and blend until soybean milk is formed. Pour milk through cloth strainer to remove residue to get 6 c. Refrigerate.

3 Bring a pot of water to boil, add somen until cooked. Drain; rinse in cold water, let cool then drain again. Divide somen to two bowls; then add cold soybean milk and shredded cucumber. This is an excellent repast during the hot Korean summers.

涼拌辣麵線

SPICY COLD NOODLES (BI BIM GUK SU)

麵線..................6 兩(225 公克)
麻油............................1 大匙
韓國泡菜、黃瓜....................
....................各 3 兩(115 公克)
牛高湯(見 8 頁)................½ 杯
西式紅椒粉、韓國辣椒粉.......
....................各 3 大匙
炒芝麻、麻油..............各 2 小匙
醬油、鹽..............各 1 小匙
蒜末.....½ 小匙，糖........5 大匙
韓國梨(切細成泥)..........6 大匙

1 泡菜切碎、黃瓜切絲；1 料仔細拌勻成麵醬，隔日味道更佳，可保存一星期。

2 多量水燒開放入麵線煮熟撈出沖水，分盛於碗內先拌麻油，依喜好上置泡菜、黃瓜及拌麵醬，食時略翻拌即可。

½ lb. (225g) somen
1 T. sesame oil
¼ lb. (115g) ea.: kimchi,
　　cucumber
½ c. beef broth, (p.8)
5 T. sugar
3 T. ea.: paprika, red pepper
　　powder
2 t. ea.: toasted sesame
　　seeds, sesame oil
1 t. ea.: soy sauce, salt
½ t. minced garlic clove
6 T. Korean pear (blended)

1 Chop kimchi and shred cucumber; mix 1 thoroughly into a thick sauce. This sauce is more flavorful if let set and refrigerated overnight. It can be kept refrigerated for 1 week.

2 Cook somen in large amount of water and drain. Rinse in cold water and drain again. Add sesame oil and toss lightly. Serve in a bowl and add kimchi, cucumber and sauce to taste. Serve.

牛尾湯麵線

OXTAIL SOMEN SOUP *(KORI GOMTANG)*

牛尾(切塊)......1½ 斤(900 公克)
① 鹽................................ 1½ 大匙
⌐ 胡椒..............................⅔ 小匙
麵線....................6 兩(225 公克)
蔥花...............................4 大匙

1 水燒開，將牛尾川燙撈出，重新放入 12 杯水煮開後，去泡沫改小火加蓋煮約 2 小時至牛尾熟爛，若剩太多湯汁中途去蓋，大火煮至牛高湯剩 7 杯，加入 ① 料，即成牛尾湯。高湯可放入冰箱，待浮油凝固後除去。

2 若要加麵線，則用多量水將麵線煮熟撈出，分盛 4 碗，再加入牛尾湯，撒上蔥花。

蘿蔔牛骨湯
將牛尾改用牛排骨、煮成牛高湯後，加白蘿蔔，並加韓國醬油、胡椒、蒜及蔥末。

2 lbs. (900g) oxtail, cut in pieces
① **1½ T. salt**
⌐ **⅔ t. pepper**
½ lb. (225g) somen
4 T. chopped green onions

1 Blanch oxtails in boiling water. Place 12 c. water in pot and boil oxtails, remove surface sediment. Reduce heat to low, cover and cook 2 hours until oxtails are tender. If too much broth remains, increase heat to high, uncover and boil until 7 c. remain. Add ① to complete the oxtail soup. To reduce fat content, place broth in refrigerator, after cooling remove surface fat.

2 If you wish to add somen, boil it in water; drain. Divide to 4 bowls. Add oxtail pieces and broth to each bowl; sprinkle with green onions.

SHORT RIBS IN BEEF BROTH *(KAI BI TANG)*
Replace oxtails with short ribs to make the beef broth. Add daikons, Korean soy sauce, pepper, minced garlic cloves, and green onions.

家常雞絲湯麵

CHICKEN NOODLE SOUP *(DAK KAL KOOK SOO)*

雞.......................................½ 隻
小馬鈴薯(切片)....................1 個
新鮮麵條...........6 兩(225 公克)
⌐ 意大利瓜(切絲)....................½ 杯
① 蒜末.....1 小匙，鹽..........1 大匙
蛋(打散).....1 個，蔥段......½ 杯

1 雞放入鍋內，加 8 杯水蓋滿過雞煮開，改小火蓋鍋煮 1½ 小時至肉熟軟；撈出去骨後肉撕成絲，留雞湯 5 杯備用。

2 將 5 杯雞湯及馬鈴薯放入鍋內，煮開後續煮 3 分鐘，放入麵條，輕輕攪動煮至麵條半熟，續放入 ① 料再煮 3 分鐘至麵熟(圖 1)，最後徐徐放入蛋液及蔥段，分盛 2 碗，上置雞絲。可與泡菜配食。

half chicken
1 small potato, sliced
½ lb. (225g) fresh noodles
⌐ **½ c. shredded zucchini**
① **1 t. minced garlic clove**
⌐ **1 T. salt**
1 beaten egg
½ c. sectioned green onions

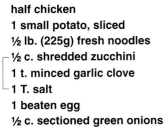

1 Immerse chicken completely in a pot with 8 c. water, bring to boil, turn to low heat and cover. Cook 1½ hours until tender. Remove chicken and shred meat, discard bones. Save 5 c. residual broth, set aside.

2 Place potato and 5 c. broth in pot. Bring to boil and cook 3 minutes. Add noodles, and stir lightly until half cooked; add ①. Cook 3 more minutes until done (Fig.1). Add beaten eggs and green onions slowly while continuing to cook. Place in 2 bowls, add chicken shreds on top and serve. Appropriate to complement with kimchi.

黃瓜泡菜
CUCUMBER KIMCHI (*O-E KIMCHI*)

小黃瓜 ....10 條

① 洋蔥、白蘿蔔、韭菜、蔥、韓
國西洋菜.............切碎共 2¼ 杯
蒜末、薑末 ....各 1 大匙

② 鹽 ....2 大匙
糖粉 ....2 小匙
韓國辣椒粉、大紅椒末..各 4 大匙

1 黃瓜選擇大小一致的，逐一切去兩端，淨重 1½ 斤(900 公克)，再切成兩半，每塊小黃瓜由切口處切十字(圖 1)。以水 4 杯拌鹽 2 大匙蓋滿黃瓜，醃 30 分鐘後瀝乾。

2 將 ① 料及 ② 料攪拌均勻，塞入黃瓜十字口內(盡量多塞)裝入瓶罐，置於室溫半天後會產生湯汁，略帶酸味，冰涼後即可食用，存放於冰箱內可保存一星期。

■ 泡菜是否美味其關鍵在於韓國辣椒粉的選擇。

10 small cucumbers

① **2¼ c.total(minced): onions, daikon, Chinese chives, green onions, Korean watercress**
1 T. ea.(minced): garlic cloves, ginger root

② **2 T. salt, 2 t. sweet & low**
4 T. ea.: red pepper powder, minced red bell pepper

1 Select cucumbers of the same size, cut off both ends so approximately 2 lbs. (900g) remain. Cut lengthwise in two. Cut a cross in each section (lengthwise); do not cut through (Fig.1). Mix 4 c.water with 2 T. of salt. Immerse cucumbers in this mixture for 30 minutes then drain.

2 Mix ① and ② then put mixture in sliced ends of cucumbers, (put as much as possible). Place cucumbers in a jar that can be sealed; leave at room temperature ½ day. Look for juice to leak from cucumbers; refrigerate. Cucumber Kimchi may be kept refrigerated for a week. Serve cold.

■ Kimchi's delightful flavor depends on the selection of red pepper powder used.

蘿蔔泡菜
RADISH KIMCHI (*KAK DU KI*)

白蘿蔔 * ....2 條

① 鹽、蔥段.....................各 3 大匙
韓國辣椒粉........................½ 杯
糖粉 ....1½ 小匙
魚露 **..........................1½ 大匙
蒜、薑末.....................各 1 大匙

1 將蘿蔔去皮切方塊(圖 2)，淨重 2 斤 4 兩 (1350 公克)，隨加 ① 料仔細拌勻裝入瓶罐內，置於室溫一天後會產生湯汁，略帶酸味，冰涼後即可食用。在冰箱內可保存一星期。

* 蘿蔔種類很多，有一種短且肥大表皮略帶綠色的品種最適宜做泡菜，一般產季在冬天。

** 韓國菜所用的魚露(圖 3)和一般泰式魚露類似。

2 daikons*

① **3 T. ea.: salt, sectioned green onions**
½ c. red pepper powder
1½ t. sweet & low
1½ T. anchovy sauce**
1 T. ea.(minced): garlic cloves, ginger root

1 Peel daikons and cut into cubes (Fig. 2) to make 3 lbs. (1350g). Mix with ① thoroughly, then place in a jar that can be sealed; let sit at room temperature for 1 day. Look for juice to leak from daikons; refrigerate. Radish kimchi can be kept refrigerated for a week. Serve cold.

* There are different kinds of daikon (white radish); there is one that is short and wide , skin is slightly greenish and is considered to be the best choice to make kimchi. It is mostly available in winter.

** Anchovy sauce used in Korean cooking (Fig.3) is similar to Thai fish sauce. If not available, Thai fish sauce may be used as a substitute.

速成泡菜
NAPA CABBAGE SALAD (KOT JUL YI)

大白菜 .... 12 兩 (450 公克)
韭菜(切段) ....¾ 杯
┌ 蒜末、鹽 ....各 ½ 大匙
│ 薑末 ....½ 小匙
│ 韓國辣椒粉 ....2 大匙
1 │ 魚露(見 77 頁,圖 3) ...1 大匙
│ 麻油 ....¾ 大匙
└ 米醋、糖 ....各 1 小匙

1 大白菜洗淨拭乾,一片片直切成 2 或 3 條或用手撕開。

2 將 1 料放入盆內拌勻,放入備好的白菜翻拌均勻,再加韭菜略拌即可。

■ 做法簡單、開胃,也可隨意灑上炒香的芝麻。

1 lb. (450g) napa cabbage
¾ c. sectioned Chinese
  chives
┌ ½ T. ea.: minced garlic
│   clove, salt
│ ½ t. minced ginger root
1 │ 2 T. red pepper powder
│ 1 T. anchovy sauce (p.77,
│   Fig.3)
│ ¾ T. sesame oil
└ 1 t. ea.: rice vinegar, sugar

1 Wash and drain cabbage. Cut or tear cabbage leaves lengthwise into two or three strips.

2 Mix 1 in a large bowl; toss napa cabbage in the bowl to mix well. Add Chinese chives and mix lightly.

■ This dish is easy to prepare and very appetizing. Sprinkle with toasted sesame seeds as desired.

蒜頭泡菜
PICKLED GARLIC (MA NUL JANG A CHI)

蒜頭 ....5 個
┌ 水 ....2½ 杯
1 │ 米醋 ....5 大匙
└ 鹽 ....1 大匙
┌ 水 ....2½ 杯
2 │ 米醋 ....5 大匙
└ 鹽、糖 ....各 1 大匙

1 將蒜頭外皮擦淨,與 1 料泡於密封的罐內,置於陰涼地方或冰箱一星期,倒出泡汁不要。

2 將 2 料煮開待冷,倒入蒜頭罐內蓋緊,醃 15 天即可食。在冰箱內可保存 6 個月。

5 garlic bulbs
┌ 2½ c. water
1 │ 5 T. rice vinegar
└ 1 T. salt
┌ 2½ c. water
2 │ 5 T. rice vinegar
└ 1 T. ea.: salt, sugar

1 Wipe off garlic without removing outer skin. Place in a jar and add 1; tighten lid. Let sit in a cool area, or refrigerate. Remove liquid after one week.

2 Bring 2 to a boil; let cool. Pour into garlic jar; tighten lid again. Soak 15 days; serve. Can be kept refrigerated for 6 months.

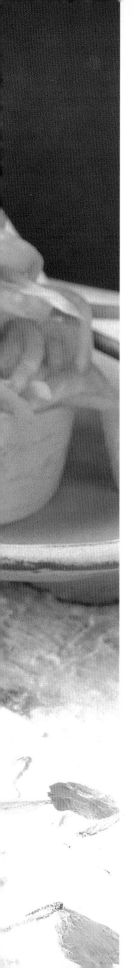

涼拌蘿蔔絲
SPICY DAIKON SALAD *(MU CHAE)*

1 ┌ 白蘿蔔絲，紅蘿蔔絲 ....
  └ ....共 8 兩 (300 公克)

2 ┌ 鹽 ....1 小匙
  │ 糖 ....4 小匙
  │ 米醋 ....1 大匙
  └ 韓國辣椒粉 ....¼ 小匙

1 將 1 料及 2 料拌勻立即可食。喜食酸味者，可多加濃縮醋少許。

■ 涼拌蘿蔔絲與涼拌黃瓜做法略不同，涼拌蘿蔔絲不需要事先用鹽醃過。

1 ┌ ⅔ lb. (300g) total
  │   (shredded): daikons,
  └   carrots

2 ┌ 1 t. salt
  │ 4 t. sugar
  │ 1 T. rice vinegar
  └ ¼ t. red pepper powder

1 Mix 1 and 2. Serve. If a strong vinegar taste is preferred, add a few drops of concentrated vinegar (gang cho).

■ Daikon Salad (Mu Chae) and Cucumber Salad (O-E Muchim) have different preparation procedures, daikon salad does not require marinating with salt in advance.

涼拌小黃瓜
SPICY CUCUMBER SALAD *(O-E MUCHIM)*

小黃瓜 ....12 兩 (450 公克)
鹽 ....1 小匙
1 ┌ 糖、韓國辣椒粉、麻油、鹽、
  │ 米醋 ....各 ½ 小匙
  └ 蒜末、芝麻 ....各 ¼ 小匙

1 小黃瓜切除兩端後切片(圖 1)，加鹽醃 30 分鐘，略沖水後擠乾水份，與 1 料拌勻即可。

1 lb. (450g) cucumber
1 t. salt
1 ┌ ½ t. ea.: sugar, red pepper
  │   powder, sesame oil, salt,
  │   rice vinegar
  │ ¼ t. ea.: minced garlic
  └   clove, sesame seeds

1 Cut off both ends of cucumber, slice (Fig. 1). Add salt, let pieces marinate 30 minutes. Rinse briefly then squeeze out water. Mix with 1; serve.

1

滷味蓮藕
LOTUS ROOTS IN SOY SAUCE *(YEUN KEUN JO RIM)*

蓮藕(去皮切片) ....2 杯

① 水..................................5 杯
醬油 ....3 大匙
玉米糖漿 ....1 小匙
糖...................................2 大匙
蒜末 ....¼ 小匙

1 蓮藕放入 ① 料內煮開(圖 1),改中火不加蓋煮 1 小時,至湯汁略收乾,熄火待冷即可食。

■ 滷味蓮藕可儲存冰箱內 1 星期。

2 c. lotus roots (peeled and sliced)

① **5 c. water**
3 T. soy sauce
1 t. corn syrup
2 T. sugar
¼ t. minced garlic clove

1. Place lotus roots in ① and bring to boil (Fig.1). Reduce heat to medium; cook uncovered one hour until liquid is almost evaporated. Let cool then serve.

■ Lotus roots may be kept fresh in the refrigerator up to one week.

涼拌豆芽
BEAN SPROUT SALAD *(SOOK JU NAMUL)*

綠豆芽 ....8 兩(300 公克)

① 鹽、麻油 ....各 ½ 小匙
蒜末 ....¼ 小匙

1 多量水燒開,放入豆芽川燙撈出沖水,用手擠乾水份,拌入 ① 料立即可食。

涼拌菠菜
菠菜川燙撈出沖水,用手擠乾水份,拌入 ① 料,可加少許糖及炒芝麻。

⅔ lb (300g), mung bean sprouts

① **½ t. ea.: salt, sesame oil**
¼ t. minced garlic clove

1 Blanch sprouts in boiling water. Rinse the sprouts in water, squeeze out excess water. Mix with ①; serve.

SPINACH SALAD *(SI KUM CHI NA MUL)*
Blanch spinach in boiling water. Rinse in water, squeeze out excess water, mix with ①. Toss with a pinch of sugar and toasted sesame seeds; serve.

辣味生蟹
SPICY CRAB (KE JANG)

活蟹 2 隻...........1 斤(600 公克)
① ┌ 醬油..................................½ 杯
  └ 牛高湯...............⅓ 杯 (見 8 頁)
  ┌ 韓國辣椒粉....................4 大匙
  │ 麻油..............................1 大匙
  │ 糖...............................2½ 大匙
② │ 炒芝麻...........................1 小匙
  │ 辣椒、蔥................切碎各 2 支
  └ 蒜....2 小匙，薑末.......½ 小匙

2 live crabs,1⅓ lb. (600g)
① ┌ **½ c. soy sauce**
  └ **⅓ c. beef broth (p.8)**
  ┌ **4 T. red pepper powder**
  │ **1 T. sesame oil**
  │ **2½ T. sugar**
② │ **1 t. toasted sesame seeds**
  │ **2 ea.(minced): Korean chili**
  │   **peppers, green onions**
  │ **2 t. minced garlic cloves**
  └ **½ t. minced ginger root**

1 蟹取下蟹蓋 (圖 1)，去鰓，刷淨外殼後切塊，蟹鉗鎚破。

2 將 ① 料煮開加 ② 料拌勻後冰涼，隨即拌入切好的蟹塊醃 24 小時即可食用，可存放於冰箱 3 天。

1 Remove shells (Fig.1) and gills from crabs; scrub shells clean. Cut crabs into pieces and crack claws.

2 Boil ① and add ②; mix well and let cool. Place crabs in this mixture for 24 hours. Serve. Can be kept refrigerated for up to three days.

牛肉涼菜
SPICY CHILLED BEEF (JANG JO RIM)

腰肉牛排..........12 兩(450 公克)
① ┌ 薑...................................3 片
  └ 水...................................5 杯
② ┌ 醬油 ....1 杯，糖...........½ 杯
  └ 蒜..................................10 個
  韓國辣椒............................5 支

1 lb.(450g) flank steak
① ┌ **3 ginger slices**
  └ **5 c. water**
② ┌ **1 c. soy sauce**
  │ **½ c. sugar**
  └ **10 garlic cloves**
  5 Korean chili peppers

1 多量水燒開，放入牛排川燙即撈出切塊(圖 2)

2 牛肉塊放入 ① 料內，蓋鍋大火煮 40 分鐘，用綿紙吸去油脂後，加 ② 料煮 20 分鐘煮至湯汁略蓋過牛肉時，即放入辣椒小火再煮 5 分鐘熄火冰涼即可。

■ 煮好的牛肉涼菜可當小菜，或做為便當菜。

1 Blanch flank steak; drain and let cool. Cut into chunks (Fig.2).

2 Place flank steak and ① in a pot. Cover and cook over high heat for 40 minutes. Place a paper towel on the liquid surface to soak off fat. Add ②, and cook for 20 minutes until liquid slightly covers the steak. Add chili peppers and simmer at low heat for 5 more minutes. Let cool or refrigerate; serve.

■ This dish can be served as a side dish.

馬鈴薯煎餅
POTATO PANCAKES (GAM JA BU CHIM)

馬鈴薯......................2 個
① 麻油......................1 小匙
└ 鹽......................½ 小匙
② 紅蘿蔔、馬鈴薯.....切絲共 ½ 杯
煎餅沾醬 (見 16 頁)

1 將馬鈴薯去皮磨碎後擠出水份，取馬鈴薯泥 1 杯，加入 ① 料，分成 8 份；② 料泡水後瀝乾 (圖 1)，分成 16 份備用。

2 油 1 大匙燒熱，先將 1 份 ② 料撒於鍋內，放上 1 份馬鈴薯泥，再加 1 份 ② 料於馬鈴薯泥上，煎至兩面金黃(煎時如有需要可加少許油) 共煎 8 片，可沾 "煎餅沾醬" 或醬油食用。

2 potatoes
① **1 t. sesame oil**
└ **½ t. salt**
② **½ c. total (shredded):**
└ **carrots, potato**
pancake sauce (p.16)

1 Peel and finely grate potatoes; squeeze out water. Place 1 c. grated potatoes in a bowl with ①. Mix well and divide into 8 portions. Soak ② in water; drain (Fig.1), then divide into 16 portions.

2 Heat 1 T. oil; sprinkle one portion of ② into frying pan. Place one portion of grated potatoes on top of ② and then add another portion of ② on top to form a "sandwich". Repeat with the remaining portions. Fry until both sides are golden brown. Add a little oil as desired when frying. Serve with pancake sauce or soy sauce as desired.

1

泡菜煎餅
KIMCHI PANCAKES (KIMCHI JUN)

① 麵粉......................1 杯
水......................½ 杯
└ 鹽......................½ 小匙
② 韓國泡菜 *(切碎)......................1 杯
蔥末......................2 大匙
蒜末......................1 小匙
└ 麻油......................2 小匙

1 拌勻 ① 料，再入 ② 料攪拌成麵糊。

2 油 2 大匙燒熱，每次 ¼ 份麵糊，放入鍋內攤平成餅狀，煎至兩面金黃，再改小火將其煎熟，共做 4 片。

★ 韓國泡菜不必洗，若怕太辣則略沖洗一下。

■ 這道菜為家常煎餅，可當鹹點或前菜。

① **1 c. all-purpose flour**
½ c. water
└ **½ t. salt**
② **1 c. minced kimchi***
2 T. minced green onion
1 t. minced garlic clove
└ **2 t. sesame oil**

1 Mix ① and combine with ② to create a thick "pancake" batter.

2 Heat 2 T. oil; place ¼ of the batter in the pan to form a "pancake". Fry until both sides are golden. Reduce heat to low and cook all the way through. Repeat with remaining portions.

★ It's unnecessary to wash kimchi; rinse it only if it is too spicy.

■ These two dishes are both very popular traditional "home style" snacks and also can be served as appetizers.

甜糯米糕
SWEET RICE CAKE (YAK SHIK)

糯米......................2 杯

① ┌ 紅糖.....½ 杯，焦糖 *.....½ 小匙
  ├ 麻油......................1 小匙
  └ 鹽......................¼ 小匙

② ┌ 栗子、紅棗(無籽)........各 15 粒
  └ 松子......................1 大匙(壓碎)

1 將糯米洗淨泡水過夜後瀝乾；蒸籠內置紗布，放入糯米以大火蒸 15 分鐘。

2 蒸過的糯米飯加入 ① 及 ② 料放入大盆內趁熱拌勻(圖 1)，倒回蒸籠再蒸 40 分鐘，取出切塊，冷或熱食均可，適合與 "甜麥芽糯米湯" (見 91 頁)當飯後甜點。

★ 糖放入乾淨的鍋內，炒成咖啡色的糖漿即為焦糖，目的是為了取其顏色。

2 c. sweet rice

① ┌ **½ c. brown sugar, ½ t. caramel***
  ├ **1 t. sesame oil**
  └ **¼ t. salt**

② ┌ **15 ea.: chestnuts, dried seedless red dates**
  └ **1 T. pine nuts (mashed)**

1 Soak sweet rice in water overnight; then drain. Place a gauze cloth in steamer; place rice on cloth and steam over high heat for 15 minutes.

2 Place sweet rice in a large bowl; add mixtures ① and ② (Fig.1) while rice is hot. Mix well, then re-steam for 40 minutes. Remove, cut into pieces and serve hot or cold, or complement with "Sweet Rice Punch"(p. 91) as a dessert.

★ Place sugar into clean frying pan, stir-fry until liquefied into caramel syrup, or purchase caramel from a market. The caramel color is essential to the presentation of this dish.

辣味米棒
HOT AND SPICY RICE CAKE (DOK BOK KI)

粘米棒 *..........12 兩(450 公克)

① ┌ 麻油......................1 小匙
  └ 韓國辣椒醬......................2 大匙

② ┌ 水......1⅓ 杯，糖..........2 小匙
  └ 韓國辣椒粉......................¼ 小匙

蔥(切段)......................1 支

1 將 ① 料放入鍋內略炒，隨入米棒及 ② 料煮開，再以小火煮至米棒熟透，煮時略攪動以免粘鍋，煮至湯汁略收，最後放入蔥段即可。

★ 粘米棒(圖 2)是用米製成的，有長短不同尺寸的米棒。若是冰凍的可放入水內解凍後再用。

1 lb. (450g) rice cake*

① ┌ **1 t. sesame oil**
  └ **2 T. hot pepper paste (go chu jang)**

② ┌ **1⅓ c. water, 2 t. sugar**
  └ **¼ t. red pepper powder**

1 green onion, sectioned

1 Lightly stir-fry ①, add rice cakes and ②; let boil. Reduce heat to low, cook until rice cake is done all the way through and juice has evaporated. While cooking, stir continuously to avoid sticking to pan. Add green onion sections and serve.

★ Rice cake (Fig.2) is made from long-grain rice; may purchase ready-made from the market. If it is frozen, you can put in water to defrost and then prepare.

柿子薑湯
PERSIMMON PUNCH (*SOO JUNG GA*)

① 薑片....................................1 杯
　肉桂條................................⅔ 杯
② 白糖.........½ 杯，紅糖........1 杯
　乾柿子................................10 個
　松子....................................1 大匙

① 1 c. ginger slices
　⅔ c. cinnamon sticks
② ½ c. white sugar
　1 c. brown sugar
　10 dried persimmons
　1 T. pine nuts

1 將 ① 料(圖 1)加水 12 杯煮開，改中火煮 2 小時後，撈出薑及肉桂不要，取 10 杯薑汁加入 ② 料燒開，煮到糖溶化熄火待涼。

2 取部份薑汁浸滿全部柿子(可整粒或切塊)；將浸泡的柿子及剩餘薑汁分別置於冰箱備用。

3 食用時每一個小碗內置柿子及薑汁，灑上少許松子即可。

1 Add ① (Fig.1) to 12 c. water, bring to boil. Reduce heat to medium and cook 2 hours. Discard ginger and cinnamon sticks. Retain 10 c. juice. Add ② and bring to boil until all sugar is dissolved.

2 Pour ginger juice so as to just cover all persimmons (can be whole or cut into pieces); place in refrigerator with leftover juice.

3 Place persimmon in each bowl, add ginger juice and pine nuts and serve.

麥芽糯米湯
SWEET RICE PUNCH (*SIK HAE*)

　糯米....................................1 杯
①｜麥芽粉(圖2)....................1½ 杯
　｜水......................................1 杯
　糖......................................6 大匙
②｜松子..................................1 大匙
　｜檸檬..................................10 片

1 c. sweet rice
①｜1½ c. barley germ powder (Fig.2)
　｜11 c. water
　6 T. sugar
②｜1 T. pine nuts
　｜10 lemon slices

1 糯米(不洗)加 1 杯水，煮成糯米飯；① 料攪拌靜置 3-4 小時後，取 10 杯麥芽汁備用，底部的沉澱物不要。

2 將糯米飯加入麥芽汁內略攪，置於電鍋內按保溫 4 小時以上，見 70% 的糯米飯浮出後，加糖略拌冰涼備用。

3 冰涼的"麥芽糯米湯"盛在碗內依隨喜好加入 ② 料當盤飾。

■ 以上二種甜點，"柿子薑湯"比"麥芽糯米湯"甜，通常適用於任何場合當甜食。

1 Add 1 c. water to unwashed sweet rice and cook. Mix ① and let sit 3 to 4 hours. Save juice (10 cups) and discard residual barley.

2 Put sweet rice with barley juice in a rice cooker, set at "warm" (not "cook") for minimum 4 hours until 70% of rice floats on top. Add sugar, stir well, then refrigerate until cold.

3 Pour iced rice punch in a bowl as desired, add ② as garnish.

■ "Sweet Rice Punch" is generally not as sweet as "Persimmon Punch," but both are popular desserts that are served at many special occasions and banquets.

養生茶
HERBAL TEAS

1 ┌ 新鮮高麗蔘......3 兩(115 公克)
　└ 甘草 * ....2 片

2 ┌ 紅棗(略洗).......6 兩(225 公克)
　└ 甘草 * ....2 片

3 ┌ 薑(略切)...........3 兩(115 公克)
　├ 甘草 * ....2 片
　└ 紅棗...................................2 個

4 ┌ 松子 ....隨意
　└ 蜂蜜 ....隨意

高麗蔘茶
將 1 料加水 7 杯煮開，不蓋鍋續煮 50 分鐘熄火，過濾後得湯汁 4 杯分盛杯內加 4 料即成。

紅棗茶
將 2 料加水 10 杯煮開，不蓋鍋續煮 50 分鐘熄火，過濾後得湯汁 4 杯分盛杯內加 4 料即成。

薑茶
將 3 料(圖 1)加水 7 杯煮開，不蓋鍋續煮 50 分鐘熄火，過濾後得湯汁 4 杯分盛杯內加 4 料即成。

* 甘草－草本植物的一種常用於中國藥膳中，主要功效為解毒降火，潤肺去痰緩和藥性。加於茶中，可增加甘甜味，易於入喉。

1 ┌ ¼ lb. (115g) fresh ginseng
　│　root
　└ 2 kam cho*

2 ┌ ½ lb. (225g) dried dates
　│　(rinsed)
　└ 2 kam cho*

3 ┌ ¼ lb. (115g) thick ginger
　│　slices
　├ 2 kam cho*
　└ 2 dried dates

4 ┌ pine nuts as desired
　└ honey as desired

GINSENG TEA (*IN SAM CHA*)
Bring 1 and 7 cups water to boil. Continue to boil for 50 minutes (uncovered), until 4 cups remain. Serve with 4.

DATE TEA (*DAE CHU CHA*)
Bring 2 and 10 cups water to boil. Continue to boil for 50 minutes (uncovered), until 4 cups remain. Serve with 4.

GINGER TEA (*SAN KANG CHA*)
Bring 3 (Fig.1) and 7 cups water to boil. Continue to boil for 50 minutes (uncovered), until 4 cups remain. Serve with 4.

*Kam cho is an herb, used frequently in Chinese herbal medicinal and health cooking. It is added in tea to enhance flavor. Kam cho is also known to soothe a sore throat and reduce coughs.

1

索引

INDEX

WEI-CHUAN COOKBOOKS

CHINESE CUISINE
APPETIZERS, CHINESE STYLE
CHINESE COOKING MADE EASY
CHINESE CUISINE
CHINESE COOKING FAVORITE HOME DISHES
CHINESE COOKING FOR BEGINNERS [1]
FISH, CHINESE STYLE MADE EASY [2]
SHELLFISH, CHINESE STYLE MADE EASY [2]

CHINESE REGIONAL CUISINE
CHINESE CUISINE, BEIJING STYLE
CHINESE CUISINE, CANTONESE STYLE
CHINESE CUISINE, SHANGHAI STYLE
CHINESE CUISINE, SZECHWAN STYLE
CHINESE CUISINE, TAIWANESE STYLE

GARNISHES
CHINESE GARNISHES [3]
GREAT GARNISHES

HEALTHFUL COOKING
CHINESE HERB COOKING FOR HEALTH
CHINESE HOME COOKING FOR HEALTH
LOW-CHOLESTEROL CHINESE CUISINE
SIMPLY VEGETARIAN
VEGETARIAN COOKING

INTERNATIONAL CUISINE
INDIAN CUISINE
JAPANESE CUISINE [4]
KOREAN CUISINE
MEXICAN COOKING MADE EASY [5]

ONE DISH MEALS FROM POPULAR CUISINES [2]
SINGAPOREAN, MALAYSIAN, & INDONESIAN CUISINE
THAI COOKING MADE EASY [6]
VIETNAMESE CUISINE

RICE & NOODLES
CHINESE RICE & NOODLES
NOODLES, CLASSICAL CHINESE COOKING
RICE, CHINESE HOME-COOKING
RICE, TRADITIONAL CHINESE COOKING

SPECIALTIES
CHINESE DIM SUM
CHINESE SNACKS, REVISED
CREATIVE CHINESE OVEN COOKING
INTERNATIONAL BAKING DELIGHTS

COMPACT COOKBOOK SERIES
BEEF [7]
CHICKEN [7]
SOUP! SOUP! SOUP!
TOFU! TOFU! TOFU!
VEGETABLES [7]
VERY! VERY! VEGETARIAN!

VIDEOS
CHINESE GARNISHES I [8]
CHINESE GARNISHES II [8]

OTHERS
CARVING TOOLS

• ALL COOKBOOKS ARE BILINGUAL (ENGLISH/CHINESE) UNLESS FOOTNOTED OTHERWISE •

1. Also available in English/Spanish, French/Chinese, and German/Chinese   2. Trilingual English/Chinese/Spanish edition
3. Bilingual English/Spanish Only   4. Also available in Chinese/French   5. Also available in English/Spanish
6. Also available in English/French   7. English and Chinese are in separate editions   8. English Only

Wei-Chuan Cookbooks can be purchased in the U.S.A., Canada and twenty other countries worldwide
1455 Monterey Pass Road, #110, Monterey Park, CA 91754, U.S.A. • Tel: (323)261-3880 • Fax: (323) 261-3299

味全叢書

中國菜系列	省份菜	拼盤·米·麵	健康系列	點心·烘焙·燒烤	異國風味	小食譜
中國菜	上海菜	拼盤與盤飾	養生藥膳	點心專輯	南洋菜	豆腐
速簡中國菜	四川菜	盤飾精選	養生家常菜	飲茶食譜	泰國菜 [4]	湯
實用中國菜 [1]	北京菜	米麵簡餐	均衡飲食	實用烘焙	越南菜	家庭素食
實用家庭菜	台灣菜	米食，家常篇	健康素	創意燒烤	印度菜	牛肉 [6]
美味小菜	廣東菜	米食，傳統篇	素食		韓國菜	雞肉 [6]
魚 [2]		麵，精華篇			日本料理 [5]	疏菜 [6]
蝦、貝、蟹 [2]					墨西哥菜 [3]	
					簡餐（五國風味） [2]	

（如無數字標註，即為中英對照版）

1．中英、英西、中法、中德版　2．中英西對照版　3．中英版及英西版　4．中英版及英法版　5．中英版及中法版　6．中文版及英文版

OTROS LIBROS DE WEI-CHUAN
EDICIONES EN ESPAÑOL
Adornos Chinos [1]
Cocina China Para Principiantes, Edición Revisada [1]
Cocina Popular de Un Solo Platillo [2]
Comida Mexicana, Fácil de Preparar [1]
Mariscos, Estilo Chino Fácil de Preparar [2]
Pescado, Estilo Chino Fácil de Preparar [2]

1. Disponible en ediciones bilingües Inglés/Español
2. Edición trilingüe Inglés/Chino/Español

Los Libros de Cocina Wei-Chuan se pueden comprar en E.E.U.U.,
Canadá y otros 20 países a través del mundo.

PLUS DE PUBLICATIONS DE WEI-CHUAN
EDITION EN FRANÇAIS
Cuisine Chinoise Pour Débutants [1]
Cuisine Thailandaise Facilitée [2]
La Cuisine Japonaise [1]

1. Edition Chinoise/Française
2. Edition Anglaise/Française

Les livres de cuisine Wei-Chuan Peuvent être achetés aux Etats-Unis,
Canada et ving autres pays du monde.